W9-ASN-818

Simple Comforts

12 COZY LAP QUILTS

Kim Diehl

Alfred Noble Library
32901 Plymouth Road
Livonia, MI 48150-1793
(734) 421-6600

Martingale ®
& COMPANY

746.46

D

AUG 2 7 2009

CREDITS

President & CEO ■ Tom Wierzbicki

Editor in Chief ■ Mary V. Green

Managing Editor ■ Tina Cook

Developmental Editor ■ Karen Costello Soltys

Technical Editor ■ Laurie Baker

Copy Editor ■ Sheila Chapman Ryan

Design Director ■ Stan Green

Production Manager ■ Regina Girard

Illustrator ■ Laurel Strand

Cover & Text Designer ■ Shelly Garrison

Photographer ■ Brent Kane

Livonia Public Library
ALFRED NOBLE BRANCH
32901 PLYMOUTH ROAD
Livonia, MI 48150-1793
734-421-6600
VO #19

MISSION STATEMENT

Dedicated to providing quality products
and service to inspire creativity.

Simple Comforts: 12 Cozy Lap Quilts
© 2009 by Kim Diehl

That Patchwork Place® is an imprint of
Martingale & Company®.

Martingale & Company
20205 144th Ave. NE
Woodinville, WA 98072-8478 USA
www.martingale-pub.com

No part of this product may be reproduced in any form, unless otherwise stated, in which case reproduction is limited to the use of the purchaser. The written instructions, photographs, designs, projects, and patterns are intended for the personal, noncommercial use of the retail purchaser and are under federal copyright laws; they are not to be reproduced by any electronic, mechanical, or other means, including informational storage or retrieval systems, for commercial use. Permission is granted to photocopy patterns for the personal use of the retail purchaser. Attention teachers: Martingale & Company encourages you to use this book for teaching, subject to the restrictions stated above.

The information in this book is presented in good faith, but no warranty is given nor results guaranteed. Since Martingale & Company has no control over choice of materials or procedures, the company assumes no responsibility for the use of this information.

Printed in China
14 13 12 11 10 09   8 7 6 5 4 3 2

Library of Congress Cataloging-in-Publication Data
Library of Congress Control Number: 2008054606

ISBN: 978-1-56477-848-2

3 9082 11320 8998

DEDICATION

To Dan, the greatest source of comfort in my life.

ACKNOWLEDGMENTS

A big thank you to Barb Stommel for suggesting the title of this book.

Many thanks to Deb Behrend, Pat Hansen, Delene Kohler, Deslynn Mecham, and Evelyne Schow for sharing your time and considerable patchwork talents.

To Celeste Freiberg, Cynthia Fuelling, and Delene Kohler, my heartfelt gratitude for your willingness to work around my hectic schedule, and especially for your beautiful machine quilting.

To Katie and Molly, my beautiful girls, thanks for hanging with me through all of the fabric shopping, straight pins, freezer paper, and miles of thread.

My sincere thanks to the talented team of people at Martingale & Company for making the preparation of this book hardly seem like work at all. To Stan Green and Brent Kane, once again you've helped me present my quilts so beautifully, and I appreciate it more than I can say. And to Laurie Baker, thanks for your endless technical knowledge, your ability to tickle my funny bone, and for making me look smart.

Many thanks to historic Gardner Village (www.gardnervillage.com) in West Jordan, Utah, for welcoming us to your beautiful and enchanting location for the photography of the quilts.

To Fairfield Processing Corporation, thank you for your yummy Soft Touch batting.

To Janome America, thank you for the use of your Memory Craft 11000 sewing machine, which makes my sewing time so much fun.

And last, my sincere thanks to Jo Morton for the sampling of your gorgeous fabrics that are sprinkled throughout the quilts in this book.

Contents

Introduction

What could be better than settling into your favorite arm chair with a good book, a refreshing drink, and the comfort of a soft and cozy quilt? I can't think of a better way to spend a quiet moment, and there are few things I love more when I'm blessed with a little unexpected time alone. Wrapping yourself within the folds of a homemade quilt is like being hugged by an old and dear friend. And like an old and dear friend, quilts only become better with time; tiny imperfections and signs of age simply show that they've been much loved and enjoyed. What greater thanks could a quiltmaker ask?

If you were to wander through my home on any given day, you would see quilts—lots of them! I love the way they lend a welcoming feel and encourage people to linger for a moment, so I use them abundantly from room to room. And while I love all of my quilts, I've come to realize that because of their size and versatility, lap quilts are my very favorites. It goes without saying that quilts grace my beds, but lap quilts adorn everything from my sofas and tabletops to my banisters and walls, and maybe even a few places in between.

Best of all, it's so easy to live with lap quilts because of the endless possibilities they bring. Simply adjusting the number of blocks and then adding or subtracting borders in any given project means that you can easily personalize your quilt to fit any area of your home. And I have to confess that few things make me happier than seeing my quilts used and enjoyed, rather than being admired from a distance. When all is said and done, who can resist seeing a happy pair of eyes peeking out from something that you've put your heart and soul into making?

Designing and sewing this collection of lap quilts has been a slice of pure pleasure for me, and knowing that they'll be enjoyed for years to come only makes them nearer and dearer to my heart. I hope these quilts will be a source of inspiration and creativity for you as well, and they'll bring a smile to the face of someone you love.

Fabric Selection

When I select my fabrics, I choose only 100%-cotton cloth of high quality. Choosing my fabrics is an important step because I believe that my fabric choices, even more than the patterns and designs, ultimately set the tone of my quilts. To simplify the process as I consider and audition my fabrics, I use the following guidelines:

- For a more traditional or formal look, I choose fewer colors and repeat them throughout the quilt top. As a general rule, I'll use just one print for each color.

- For a bit of the "make-do" look, I first select the prints that I'd like for my main color scheme, and then add several look-alikes to imply that I ran short of my original selection and had to substitute others. This method helps to ensure my choices are successful when there are several "perfect" prints I'm considering.

- To achieve a planned scrappy look, I select my colors and prints as I would for a "make-do" quilt, and then add several lighter, brighter, and deeper shades, along with a few complementary colors. I vary the size and scale of my prints for added interest, but I make sure that my choices work well together and appear deliberate.

- For a completely scrappy look, I love to take the above guidelines one step further by including colors and prints that are slightly off, but not glaringly so. It's easy to incorporate many prints by deciding at the start of your project whether your colors will be muted and slightly muddy, or if you'd prefer clear, bright tones. Once you've made this decision, nearly any print and color can be mingled successfully.

PIN POINT

Color Values

Remember that the value of any print can change depending upon the colors that are positioned immediately next to it. If I decide to work a light print into a quilt top that largely features darker tones, I will position it next to a medium-toned print to minimize the difference. The medium print acts as a bridge to blend the surrounding colors, and the lighter print adds interest without distracting from the overall look of the quilt.

My favorite method for auditioning my fabrics is to toss them in a pile on the floor, and then step back and view them from a short distance. If one fabric consistently acts as a bull's-eye, regardless of how it's mingled with the others, I remove it from my mix.

I hope that these guidelines will be helpful to you as you make your own choices. But remember that ultimately, you should listen to your instincts and always please yourself.

Quiltmaking Principles

The topics that follow provide the techniques and procedures used to piece and assemble the projects in this book. Some of these time-honored procedures are commonly practiced while others are my own methods, developed as I was teaching myself the art of quiltmaking.

YARDAGE REQUIREMENTS

The project instructions in this book assume a 42" useable width of fabric after prewashing and removing selvages. To make the best use of your yardage, always cut your pieces in the order given.

ROTARY CUTTING

Unless otherwise noted, cut all pieces on the straight of grain and across the width of the fabric. To speed the cutting process, I fold my pressed fabric in half with the selvages together, and then in half once more. This method results in four pieces with each cut. Of course, the size of the pieces will determine how many folds you can make.

Place the folded fabric on your cutting mat, aligning the folded edge with a horizontal line on the marked grid. Position your ruler on top of the fabric and make a vertical cut along one side to establish a straight edge. Measure and cut your pieces from this edge.

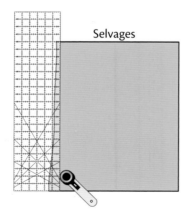

Selvages

To cut half-square triangles from a square (or layered stack of squares), lay your ruler diagonally across the square, with the cutting edge directly over the corners, and make the cut.

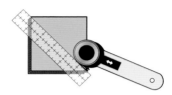

PINNING

I recommend pinning your layered patchwork pieces together at regular intervals, including all sewn seams and intersections. A good tip for sewing a consistently straight seam to the back edge of your patchwork is to pin the pieces with glass-head pins. The pin heads can be used to steer the patchwork through the machine in a straight line, eliminating inaccurate seams at the tail end where fishtailing often occurs.

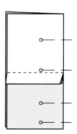

MACHINE PIECING

Unless otherwise instructed, always join your fabrics with right sides together using a ¼" seam allowance. To achieve an accurate seam allowance, I suggest using a ¼" presser foot made specifically for quilt-making. You can also make a guide using masking tape. To do this, gently lower your sewing-machine needle until the point rests upon the ¼" line of an acrylic ruler. After ensuring that the ruler is resting in a straight position, apply a line of ¼" masking tape to the sewing-machine surface exactly along the ruler's edge, taking care not to cover the feed dogs. Align the edge of the fabrics with this taped line as you feed the pieces through the machine.

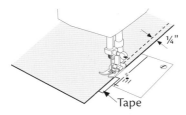

Your machine's standard stitch length will be fine for most projects. However, for smaller-scale patchwork pieces, I recommend reducing your stitch length slightly to achieve a secure seam to the very edges of your joined pieces.

PIN POINT

Threading Your Sewing Machine

Before threading your sewing machine, remember to lift your presser foot and position it in the upright position with the needle at the highest point. This will allow your thread to easily slide through all of the machine's mechanisms and speed the process.

STRIP PIECING

Several projects in this book call for strips of fabric to be sewn into sets, which are then crosscut into measured segments. I recommend pressing the seam allowance of each new strip as it is added, referring to the pattern instructions. After the strip set is pressed, position it squarely on the cutting mat. Align a horizontal line on your ruler with a seam line and cut through the strip set at one end to establish a straight edge. Measure and cut your segments from this edge.

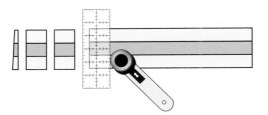

CHAIN PIECING

For projects with many pieces to be joined, chain piecing saves both time and thread. To chain piece, simply feed your patchwork units through the sewing machine one after another without snipping the threads between each. When you finish sewing, cut the threads connecting the units and press as instructed.

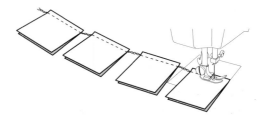

PRESSING SEAMS

Pressing well is crucial for patchwork that fits together properly. The following steps outline my pressing method.

1. Place the patchwork on a firm-surfaced ironing board, with the fabric you wish to press toward (usually the darker fabric) on top. On the wrong side of the fabric, briefly bring a hot, dry iron down onto the sewn seam to warm the fabric.

2. Lift the iron and fold the top piece of fabric back to expose the right sides of the fabrics. While the fabric is still warm, run your fingernail along the sewn thread line to relax the fibers at the fold. Press the seam flat from the right side of the patchwork. The seam allowance will lie under the fabric that was originally positioned on top.

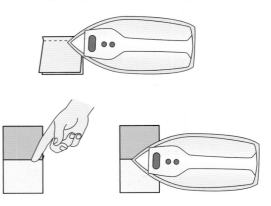

I suggest avoiding the use of steam while your blocks are being pieced and assembled because it can be difficult to make adjustments to your seams if there are blocks that require unsewing.

PRESSING TRIANGLE UNITS

Several projects in this book call for stitch-and-fold triangle units that are created by layering a square with a drawn diagonal line on top of a second square or rectangle. After stitching the pair together on the line, I recommend the following steps:

1. Fold the top triangle back and align its corner with the corner of the bottom piece of fabric to keep it square; press in place.

2. Trim away the excess layers of fabric beneath the top triangle, leaving a ¼" seam allowance.

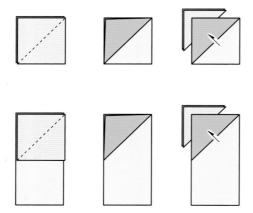

The seam allowances of triangle units are commonly trimmed *before* they are pressed, but I've found that this pressing method produces accurate patchwork that seldom requires squaring up.

PIN POINT

Smooth Pressing

Consider purchasing an iron with a nonstick surface for pressing your patchwork. The iron will glide smoothly across your fabrics, and the surface will remain in good, clean condition for longer periods of time.

Travel-sized irons are also an excellent choice for your sewing room because they use less power and aren't as heavy.

PIN POINT

Trimming Tip

When I trim away the excess layers of cloth underneath the top patchwork triangle, I routinely leave a scant ¼" seam allowance. This reduces bulk near the seam and makes hand quilting easier for projects that will be stitched ¼" out from the seam lines.

APPLIQUÉ METHODS

If you admire appliqué quilts but are a bit hesitant to make them, I encourage you to give my timesaving machine- or hand-appliqué methods a try.

Invisible Machine Appliqué

In addition to your standard quiltmaking supplies, the following tools and products are needed for this method.

- .004 monofilament thread in smoke and clear colors

- Awl or stiletto tool

- Bias bars of various widths

- Embroidery scissors with a fine, sharp point

- Liquid fabric basting glue, water-soluble and acid-free (my favorite brand is Quilter's Choice Liquid Basting Glue by Beacon Adhesives)

- Freezer paper

- Iron with a sharp pressing point (travel-sized or mini appliqué irons work well for this technique)

- Open-toe presser foot

- Sewing machine with adjustable tension control, capable of producing a tiny zigzag stitch

- Size 75/11 machine quilting needles

- Tweezers with rounded tips

Choosing Your Monofilament Thread

There are currently two types of monofilament thread available that work well for invisible machine appliqué: nylon and polyester. Both types of thread have their own characteristics and strengths and can bring different benefits to your appliqué projects.

In my experience, nylon thread tends to produce results that are slightly more invisible, but extra care should be used as your project is being assembled and pressed. For best results when working with this type of thread, avoid applying prolonged or high heat directly to the front of your appliqués and press any nearby seams carefully, because the very high degree of heat produced by an iron can weaken the nylon monofilament. Once the project is finished and bound, I find that the stitched appliqués stand up well to everyday use and care. When I use nylon monofilament for my own projects, I've had very good results using the YLI brand.

If you would like an extra measure of confidence that your appliqués will remain securely in place, even if they're inadvertently pressed from the front of your work, you may wish to use polyester monofilament thread. Depending upon the brand you choose, this thread can be slightly more visible once your appliqués have been stitched, but it will withstand a higher degree of heat as you're pressing and assembling your project. For projects where I've opted to use a polyester product, I've been very pleased with my results using the Sulky brand.

Ultimately, I recommend that you experiment with both types of monofilament and make this decision based upon your own personal results and preferences.

Preparing Pattern Templates

When a project features multiple appliqués made from any one pattern, I like the convenience of tracing around a cardboard-weight template to make the required number of pattern pieces, rather than tracing over the pattern sheet numerous times. Templates are easy to make, and as you prepare them, keep in mind that any shape can be modified to fit your skill level. To do this, simply fatten thin points and plump narrow inner curves—your pattern will look essentially the same, but you'll find the shape is much easier to work with.

1. Cut a piece of freezer paper about twice as large as your shape. Use a pencil to trace the pattern onto one end of the non-waxy side of the paper. Fold the freezer paper in half, waxy sides together, and use a hot, dry iron to fuse the folded paper into one cardboard-weight layer.

2. Cut out the shape exactly on the drawn line, taking care to duplicate it accurately.

Preparing Paper Pattern Pieces

Always cut paper pattern pieces exactly on the drawn lines; you'll add the seam allowances later as you cut your shapes from fabric. To achieve smooth pattern edges, move the paper, rather than the scissors, as you take long cutting strokes.

Use the prepared template (or pattern sheet, if you are preparing just a few pieces) to trace the specified number of pattern pieces onto the non-waxy side of a piece of freezer paper. To save time when many pieces are required, stack the freezer paper four to six pieces deep (with the waxy sides facing down), pin the layers, and cut several at once.

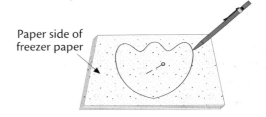

Paper side of freezer paper

Prepare mirror-image pieces by tracing the pattern onto one end of a strip of freezer paper, and then folding it accordion style in widths to fit your shape. Pin the layers together and cut out the shape. When you separate the pieces, every other shape will be a mirror image.

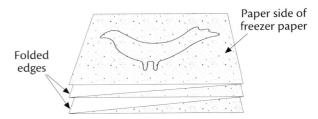

Folded edges

Paper side of freezer paper

Preparing Appliqués

1. Apply a small amount of glue from a fabric glue stick to the *non-waxy* side of each pattern piece and affix it to the wrong side of your fabric, leaving approximately ½" between each shape for seam allowances. I've found that it's best to position the longest lines or curves on the diagonal, because bias edges are easier to manipulate than straight-grain edges when pressing the seam allowances over onto the paper pattern pieces.

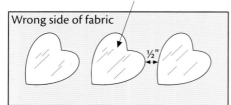

Waxy side of freezer paper up

Wrong side of fabric

½"

2. Using embroidery scissors, cut out each shape, adding a scant ¼" seam allowance around the paper.

   - Clip the seam allowance of all shapes with pronounced curves, stopping two or three threads away from the paper edge (this will preserve an intact fabric edge when the seam allowance is pressed onto the waxy side of the paper pattern piece). Larger shapes or shapes with gently flowing curves will require few (if any) clips—you'll get a feel for what works best for you as you begin working with various shapes.

   - Outer seam allowance points do not require clipping, so an unclipped area leading up to each side of a point is fine.

   - Clip inner points, such as the one at the top of a heart shape, nearly to the paper edge, taking care not to clip into the paper.

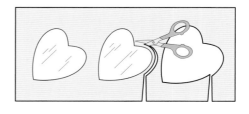

Clip inner points to paper edge.

Stop each clip for pronounced curves 2 or 3 threads from paper edge.

Pressing Appliqués

Shapes that are pressed well are easy to work with, resulting in finished appliqués that appear hand stitched. Use the steps that follow to press the seam allowance of each appliqué, keeping the edge you are working with furthest from you at approximately the twelve o'clock to one o'clock position.

NOTE: If you are right handed, work around the shape from right to left as you press, rotating the appliqué clockwise in small increments to keep the area you are pressing at the top of the shape. If you are left handed, simply reverse the directions to press and rotate the appliqué.

1. Use the point of a hot, dry iron to press the seam allowance over onto the waxy side of the pattern piece, beginning at a straight or gently curved edge and working your way around the entire shape. To avoid puckered appliqué edges, always direct the seam allowance toward the center of the shape by drawing it slightly back toward the last section pressed. You'll find it helpful to use the point of an awl or a seam ripper to grab and manipulate the fabric on smaller shapes, particularly when pressing points.

Direct seam allowance toward center of shape.

2. For sharp outer points, press the seam allowance so the folded edge of the fabric extends beyond the first side of the pattern point. Fold over the seam allowance on the remaining side of the point and continue pressing. Apply a small amount of glue stick to the inside fold of fabric at the point. Use the point of an awl or seam ripper to drag the fabric fold in and away from the appliqué edge (if necessary) and touch it with the point of a hot iron to heat set the glue and fuse the seam allowance in place.

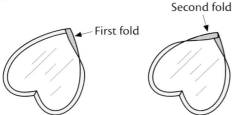

Second fold

First fold

3. To prepare a sharp inner point, use a sweeping motion to press the seam allowance leading up to the point onto the waxy side of the pattern piece. Pull the seam allowance on the remaining side of the point over onto the waxed paper and follow with the point of the iron.

Always turn your prepared appliqué over to evaluate your pressing. From the back, loosen any pressed edges that aren't smooth, and re-press. Tiny imperfections don't require re-pressing and can usually be nudged into place with the point of your iron.

PIN POINT

Achieving Smoothly Pressed Appliqués

Over the course of pressing thousands of appliqué shapes, I've found that smoothly pressed edges are easiest to achieve when you use the pad of your finger to smooth the fabric seam allowance over onto the paper pattern piece. Using the pad of your finger enables you to feel the slightly raised paper edge, and the pattern piece is less likely to fold in upon itself as you work with the shape.

Making Bias-Tube Stems and Vines

For easily prepared stems and vines that don't require the seam allowances to be turned under, I use bias tubes. Cut the fabric strips as specified in the project instructions and prepare them as follows:

1. With *wrong* sides together, fold the strip in half lengthwise and stitch a scant ¼" from the long raw edges to form a tube. For narrow stems, you'll want to trim the seam allowance to ⅛" so that it will not be visible from the front.

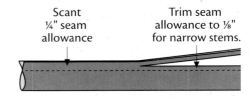

Scant ¼" seam allowance

Trim seam allowance to ⅛" for narrow stems.

2. Insert a bias bar into the tube and slide it along as you press the stem flat, centering the seam allowance so it will be hidden when you turn the stem to the front. Remove the bias bar.

Bias bar

PIN POINT

Selecting a Bias-Bar Width

The instructions for each individual project will provide the mathematically correct size of the bias bar needed, but ultimately, due to the variances that can occur as your seam allowances are sewn, I recommend that you simply choose a width that will slide easily through the tube.

3. Place *tiny* dots of liquid basting glue at approximately 1" intervals under the bottom layer of the seam allowance; use a hot dry iron to heat set the glue and fuse the seam allowance in place.

Basting Appliqués

Invisible machine appliqué, like hand appliqué, is sewn in layers from the bottom to the top.

1. Before you begin stitching, lay out the prepared appliqués on the background fabric to ensure that everything fits and is to your liking. Remember that any appliqué with a raw edge that will be overlapped by another piece (such as a stem) should be well overlapped, generally about ¼", to prevent fraying.

PIN POINT

Positioning Appliqués

When positioning your appliqués for stitching, always leave approximately ½" between the appliqués and the raw edge of the block background. This will ensure that you preserve an intact margin of space around each piece, even after the quilt top has been pieced together.

2. Remove all but the bottom appliqués and baste them in place using pins (taking care not to place them in the path of your stitching) *or* with liquid basting glue. Liquid basting glue is my preferred method because there are no pins to stitch around or remove and the appliqués will not shift as they are stitched.

To glue baste an appliqué, anchor it to the background using a single pin at the center of the shape. Fold back one half of the shape to expose the pressed seam allowance and place tiny dots of liquid glue on the fabric at approximately 1" intervals; unfold and press the glue-basted portion firmly back in place. Repeat with the remaining half of the appliqué and remove the pin.

Preparing Your Sewing Machine

For results that are nearly invisible, monofilament thread is the best choice for stitching the appliqués in place. When selecting your monofilament color, match it to the appliqué, not the background. Generally, smoke-colored thread is best for medium and dark prints and clear thread for bright or pastel hues. If the spool pin on your machine will allow the monofilament thread to stand upright, choose this position because it will help regulate the tension as the thread feeds through the needle.

1. Use a size 75/11 quilting needle in your sewing machine and thread it with monofilament.

2. Wind the bobbin with standard neutral-colored thread or thread to match your background.

   NOTE: If your machine's bobbin case features a special eye for use with embroidery techniques, threading your bobbin thread through this opening will often provide additional tension control to perfectly regulate your stitches.

3. Program your sewing machine to the zigzag stitch, adjust the width and length to achieve a tiny stitch as shown below, and reduce the tension setting. For many sewing machines, a width, length, and tension setting of 1 produces the perfect stitch.

Approximate stitch size

Stitching the Appliqués

Before stitching your first invisible-machine-appliqué project, I recommend experimenting with a simple pattern shape to become comfortable with this technique and to find the best settings for your sewing machine.

PIN POINT

Preparing an Appliqué Reference Sample

After stitching your practice appliqué, keep it on hand for use as a quick reference for future projects. Make a note directly on the background area of your sewn sample as to your machine's width, length, and tension settings, and even whether your machine begins zigzag stitching on the left- or right-hand side. This will save lots of time when you begin new projects, and you'll never need to rely on your memory!

1. Slide the basted appliqué under the sewing-machine needle from front to back to direct the threads behind the machine.

2. If your machine begins zigzag stitching on the left, position the background so the needle will pierce the appliqué just inside the prepared edge. If your machine begins zigzag stitching on the right, position the background so the needle will pierce the fabric next to the appliqué when it is lowered. Place your fingertip over the monofilament tail and hold it in place to prevent thread snarls while the machine takes two or three locking stitches. If your machine does not offer a locking-stitch feature, reduce the stitch length to the shortest setting and take two or three small stitches in place, *or* ensure that your starting stitches are overlapped by approximately 1" as you finish stitching.

3. Lift your fingertip from the monofilament and begin zigzag stitching so that the inner stitches land a couple of threads inside the appliqué and the outer stitches drop into the background fabric exactly next to the appliqué. I recommend watching the outer stitches while you sew to keep them positioned correctly, and the inner stitches will naturally fall into place. After stitching a short distance, pause and carefully clip the monofilament tail close to the background.

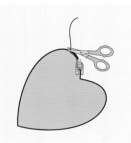

Stitch curved appliqués at a slow to moderate speed to maintain control as you steer the shape under the needle. Gently swivel the background as you stitch, stopping and pivoting as often as needed to keep the edge of the appliqué feeding straight toward the needle. I like to pivot with the needle down in the appliqué, because the paper pattern piece stabilizes the shape and keeps it from stretching.

- If dots of bobbin thread show on the *front* of your appliqué as you stitch, further adjust the tension settings on your machine (usually lower) until they disappear.

- If monofilament thread is visible underneath your appliqué from the back, or the stitches appear loose, adjust the tension settings (usually higher) until they are secure.

4. To firmly secure an inner point, stitch to the position where the inner stitch rests exactly on the inner point of the appliqué and stop. Pivot the fabric so the appliqué inner point is at a right angle to the needle; the next stitch will pierce the background. You may wish to pivot and stitch

twice to secure this delicate area. After ensuring the appliqué edge is properly aligned under the presser foot, continue stitching.

 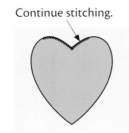

Stop and pivot. Continue stitching.

5. To secure an outer point, stitch to the position where the outer stitch lands exactly outside the appliqué point and pierces the background, and stop. Pivot the background so the unsewn edge of the appliqué is aligned to feed under the presser foot. As you begin sewing again, a second stitch will drop into the point of the appliqué, often into your last stitch.

Stop and pivot. Continue stitching.

6. Continue stitching around the perimeter of the appliqué until you overlap your starting point by approximately ¼" to ½". End with a locking stitch, or take two or three straight stitches in place. Carefully clip the thread tails.

NOTE: Your locking stitches can be placed within the appliqué or on the background. I position my starting and stopping points where the fabric's print will disguise them best.

String Appliqué

When two or more appliqués are in close proximity on the same layer, I recommend using my string appliqué method to speed the sewing process and save thread.

1. Stitch your first appliqué as instructed in "Stitching the Appliqués" on page 15, but instead of clipping the threads when you finish, lift the presser foot and slide the background to the next appliqué without lifting it from the sewing-machine surface. Lower the presser foot and resume stitching, remembering to begin and end with a locking stitch.

2. Remove your work from the sewing machine after the cluster of appliqués has been stitched and carefully clip the threads between each.

PIN POINT

Thread Tails

As you work with monofilament thread, you'll find that leaving a long thread tail during the stitching process will help keep this springy thread from drawing back up into the machine and out of the eye of the needle. For the same reason, I also suggest that you avoid using the automatic thread-cutting feature on your machine.

Removing Paper Pattern Pieces

1. On the wrong side of the appliqué, use embroidery scissors to carefully pinch and cut through the fabric at least ¼" inside the appliqué seam, taking care not to puncture the freezer paper. Trim away the background fabric, leaving a generous ¼" seam allowance. Trimming away the background, rather than cutting a slit, will result in finished appliqués that are sturdy and secure without adding bulk, especially for layered designs.

2. Grasp the appliqué edge between the thumb and forefinger of one hand and the appliqué seam allowance with the thumb and forefinger of your other hand; give a gentle but firm tug to free the edge of the paper pattern piece. Use the tip of your finger to loosen the glue where the pattern piece is anchored to the fabric. Peel away and discard the paper. If any paper remains in the appliqué corners, use a pair of tweezers to carefully remove it. It isn't necessary to remove any bits of paper that are too tiny to see or grasp easily.

NOTE: It isn't necessary to cut away the background of any appliqué that doesn't contain paper, such as a stem.

PIN POINT

Another Use for Tweezers

If your sewing machine doesn't feature an automatic needle threader, keep your tweezers handy as you thread your machine. After a tiny length of thread is through the eye of the needle, use the tweezers to grasp the end of the thread and pull it well through the opening.

Completing the Machine-Appliqué Process

Working from the bottom layer to the top, continue basting and stitching the appliqués until each one has been stitched in place. Remember to remove the paper pattern pieces before adding each new layer! Also,

keep in mind that it's not necessary to stitch any edge that will be overlapped by another appliqué. If necessary, lay your completed work face down on your ironing board and lightly and *briefly* press it from the wrong side to ensure the seam allowances lie smooth and flat. Take care not to apply prolonged or high heat to the appliqués, particularly from the front, because this can weaken the monofilament threads.

Turn-Free Hand Appliqué

If you love hand sewing or just like the option of on-the-go needlework, the following technique will help you prepare portable projects. In addition to the items outlined in "Invisible Machine Appliqué" on page 10, you'll need these supplies:

- Fine-gauge thread in a variety of colors to match your appliqués
- Straw appliqué needles (size 9 or 10 work well for me)
- Thimble

Preparing and Stitching the Appliqués

1. Prepare the appliqués using freezer paper as outlined in "Invisible Machine Appliqué" on page 10.

2. After laying out the prepared appliqués on the background, remove all but the bottom appliqués. Baste them in place as instructed in "Basting Appliqués" on page 14.

3. Cut a length of thread in a color to match the appliqué and insert one end through the eye of the needle. To tie a knot, form a small loop near the tail end of the thread, rolling it between your thumb and forefinger two or three times to draw the end through the opening. Pull the loop tight to form a knot.

4. Bring the needle up from the wrong side of the background, just inside the appliqué, catching two or three threads along the appliqué edge. Pull the thread until the knot is flush with the fabric.

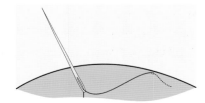

5. Insert the needle into the background just behind the point where the thread exits the fabric and come back up through the appliqué a tiny distance in front of your last stitch, again just catching the threads along the appliqué edge. Gently pull the thread until the stitch is secure. Continue stitching around the appliqué in this manner, taking close, tiny stitches to secure it firmly to the background. Sewing small, sturdy stitches will ensure that the appliqué remains secure when you remove the paper pattern piece.

    NOTE: As you come to a point or corner in an appliqué shape, take two stitches to fasten the edge securely to the background.

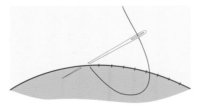

6. When you return to your starting point, insert the needle and bring it out on the wrong side of the background. Take two or three small backstitches just inside the appliqué edge, drawing the thread through the loop each time to secure it and keep it well hidden under the appliqué. (Threads that are tied off under the background fabric can create a shadow effect through fine or light-hued fabrics.) Carefully clip the thread tail.

7. Referring to "Removing Paper Pattern Pieces" on page 16, carefully remove the freezer paper.

Completing the Hand-Appliqué Process

Remember to work from the bottom layer to the top when stitching your appliqués and don't forget to remove the paper pattern pieces before adding each new layer. If necessary, lay the completed piece face down on a towel and lightly press it from the wrong side.

COMPLETING THE QUILT TOP

Once your blocks or units are completed, assembling them and adding borders is the next step. Here are some things to remember as you get closer to completing your quilt.

Assembling the Quilt Center

I recommend using a design wall or a large area of floor space to lay out your blocks and evaluate your balance of color. To define and visually anchor the quilt center, I suggest positioning blocks or units with strong hues in the corners.

For greater ease when assembling large tops, join the rows in groups of two or three. Next, join the grouped rows, working from opposite ends toward the middle, until you join the two halves.

Adding Borders

Patchwork borders contain numerous pieces or pieced units that are joined together to achieve a designated length, while whole-cloth borders are cut from one length of fabric. All of the border measurements in this book are mathematically correct, but because there is little or no stretch to whole-cloth borders cut from the lengthwise grain, you may wish to slightly increase the designated lengths for greater ease when pinning and sewing. I routinely increase the length of my strips by ½" for borders measuring up to 60" long and by 1" for strips in excess of 60". Any excess length can be trimmed after the borders are added.

When joining border strips to the center of a quilt, fold each border piece in half to find the midpoint, and then finger-press a crease. Next, fold each side of the quilt center and crease the midpoint position. Line up the creases and pin for a perfect fit.

FINISHING TECHNIQUES

There are many choices available for finishing your quilt, and your decisions will enable you to tailor the appearance of your project to suit your individual preferences.

Batting

For a contemporary look, polyester batting has minimal shrinkage after washing and is a good choice when paired with prewashed fabrics. If you prefer a softly puckered, old-fashioned look, try combining thin cotton batting with fabrics that haven't been prewashed. Always follow the manufacturer's instructions for the batting you choose.

Backing

I cut and piece my quilt backings to be 3" to 4" larger than the quilt top on all sides. When you choose your backing fabric, remember that busy prints will make your quilting less visible, while muted prints and solids will emphasize your quilting design. To prevent shadowing, use fabrics in colors similar to those in your quilt top.

For the best use of yardage, seam your quilt backings as follows.

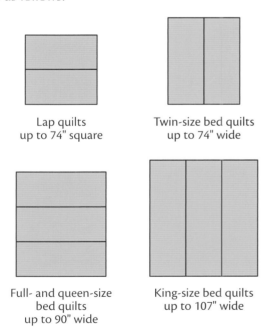

Lap quilts
up to 74" square

Twin-size bed quilts
up to 74" wide

Full- and queen-size
bed quilts
up to 90" wide

King-size bed quilts
up to 107" wide

Basting

To prepare your finished top for the quilting process:

1. Place the backing fabric, wrong side up, on a large, flat surface. Smooth any wrinkles and secure the edges with masking tape.

2. Center the batting on the backing fabric and smooth any wrinkles.

3. Carefully center the quilt top on the layered batting and backing.

   • For hand quilting, baste from corner to corner using white thread (colored thread can leave tinted fibers). Next, baste vertically and horizontally at 3" to 4" intervals. Finish by basting around the outer edges.

   • For machine quilting, place size 2 rustproof safety pins 4" to 5" apart, beginning in the center and working out toward the edges. Hand baste around the outer edges.

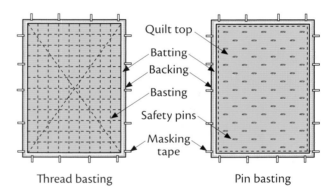

Quilt top
Batting
Backing
Basting
Safety pins
Masking
tape

Thread basting

Pin basting

Marking Quilting Designs

If you plan to outline existing shapes or stitch in the ditch (along the seam line), it may not be necessary to mark your quilting design. You can use various widths of masking tape as a guide for stitching straight lines or background grids, but remember to remove the tape at the end of each day to prevent adhesive from damaging the fabric. More elaborate designs should be marked onto the top before you assemble the layers using a quilter's silver pencil or a fine-tipped water-soluble marker. To ensure the lines can be removed, always test your water-soluble marker on a fabric swatch before marking your top.

PIN POINT

Achieving Balance in Your Quilting Designs

As a general rule, I've discovered that a nice balance can be achieved in the look of your quilting when you stitch curved designs onto borders that frame quilt centers featuring predominantly straight lines. Consequently, for quilt centers with curved shapes or quilting motifs, border designs such as cross-hatching or repeated straight lines lend a sense of order.

Whether you choose to hand or machine quilt, ensure that your project includes an adequate amount of quilting. Beautiful quilting can elevate the status of even the simplest quilt, while the most striking quilt will suffer in appearance if the quilting is scant.

Quilting

Quilting stitches are more than simply the glue that holds the layers together; they're the crowning touch on your project. Choose your favorite method or even try different methods in combination to add an unexpected design element.

Hand Quilting

To hand quilt your project, place the quilt in a hoop or frame and follow these steps:

1. Tie a knot in the end of a length of quilting thread approximately 18" long and insert the needle into the quilt top approximately 1" from where you wish to begin quilting.

2. Slide your needle through the layers and bring it up through the quilt top, gently tugging until the knot pops into the batting between the layers of fabric.

3. Make small, even stitches, taking care to stitch through all layers.

4. As you near the end of the thread, make a knot about 1/8" from the quilt top and insert the needle, sliding it through the batting only. Bring the needle up through the top about 1" beyond your last

stitch, tugging gently until the knot disappears; carefully clip the thread.

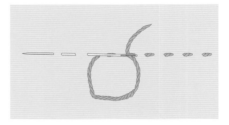

Hand-quilting stitch

Big-Stitch Quilting

The big-stitch style of hand quilting is one of my favorites. A stitch length of 1/8" to 1/4" is perfectly acceptable, making it a quick way to achieve a hand-sewn look without the investment of time that traditional hand quilting requires. Use a size 5 embroidery needle with #8 or #12 perle cotton to sew a running stitch through the layers, beginning and ending your stitches as you would for traditional hand quilting.

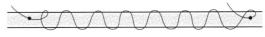

Machine Quilting

For detailed machine-quilting instructions, refer to *Machine Quilting Made Easy!* by Maureen Noble (Martingale & Company, 1994).

I have many of my projects machine quilted in a swirling design I created as an alternative to stippling. It's a wonderful choice as an overall quilting pattern or as a filler for background areas, and I've even had it stitched on top of appliqué motifs with great results.

Swirls are a wonderful overall quilting pattern.

To create this versatile design, sew a free-form circle of any size, and then fill in the center with ever-reducing concentric circles (think cinnamon rolls). When you arrive at the center, stitch a gentle wavy line to the next area you want to swirl and continue until the block or top is complete. I find that this design looks best when the swirls are staggered slightly, because this will ensure they don't cover the surface of your top in straight, even rows.

Start here.

Binding

A traditional French-fold binding made from 2½"-wide strips is commonly used to finish most quilts. When I bind my quilts, however, I prefer a more unconventional method using 2"-wide strips that results in a traditional look from the front while producing a "chubby" border of color to frame the backing. The yardages for each project will accommodate either method, with enough binding to encircle the quilt perimeter plus approximately 10" for mitered corners.

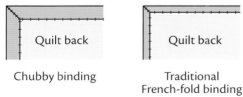

Quilt back — Chubby binding

Quilt back — Traditional French-fold binding

Traditional French-Fold Binding

1. With right sides together, join the 2½"-wide strips end to end at right angles, stitching diagonally across the corners, to make one long strip. Trim the seam allowances to ¼" and press them open.

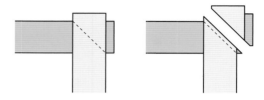

2. Cut one end at a 45° angle and press it under ¼". Fold the strip in half lengthwise, wrong sides together, and press. If the quilt will include a hanging sleeve for display purposes, refer to "Making a Hanging Sleeve" on page 23 and add it prior to binding the quilt. The binding will encase the raw edges of the sleeve.

Fold line

3. Beginning along one side of the quilt top, not a corner, use a ¼" seam to stitch the binding along the raw edges. Stop sewing ¼" from the first corner and backstitch. Clip the thread and remove the quilt from under the presser foot.

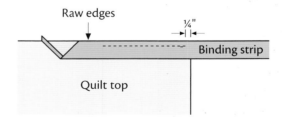

Raw edges

¼"

Binding strip

Quilt top

4. Make a fold in the binding, bringing it up and then back down onto itself to square the corner. Rotate the quilt 90° and reposition it under the

presser foot. Resume sewing at the top edge of the quilt, continuing around the perimeter in the same manner.

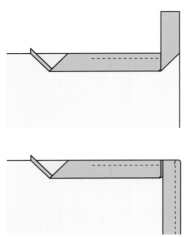

5. When you approach your starting point, cut the end at an angle 1" longer than needed and tuck it inside the previously sewn binding to enclose the raw end. Complete the stitching.

6. Bring the folded edge of the binding to the back of the quilt, enclosing the raw edges. Use a blind stitch and matching thread to hand sew the binding to the back. At each corner, fold the binding to form a miter and stitch it in place.

PIN POINT

Erasing Iron Build-Up

If your iron doesn't feature a nonstick pressing surface and it begins to show signs of residue build-up, here's a little trick to spruce it up. Unplug the iron and let it rest until the pressing surface is cool to the touch. Next, gently rub a dampened Mr. Clean Magic Eraser over the plate to remove any build-up; wipe thoroughly with a clean dry cloth.

"Chubby" Binding

For this method, you'll need a bias-tape maker designed to produce 1"-wide, double-fold tape. For most of my quilts, I prefer to use binding strips cut on the straight of grain, rather than the bias, because I feel this gives my quilt edges more stability. For scrappy bindings pieced from many lengths, I usually join the strips end to end using a straight seam and start with a straight rather than diagonal fold at the beginning.

1. Cut the strips 2" wide and join them end to end.

2. Slide the pieced strip through the bias-tape maker, pressing the folds with a hot iron as they emerge so the raw edges meet in the center. As the tape emerges from the tape maker, the seams where the strips are joined will automatically be pressed to one side.

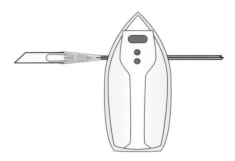

3. Open the fold of the strip along the top edge only. Turn the beginning raw end under ½" and finger-press. Starting along one side of the quilt top, not a corner, align the unfolded raw edge of the binding with the raw edge of the quilt and stitch as instructed in steps 3 and 4 of the French-fold method on page 21.

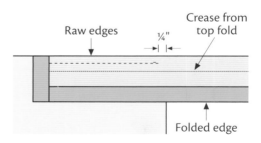

Raw edges   ¼"   Crease from top fold

Folded edge

4. When you approach your starting point, cut the end to extend 1" beyond the folded edge and complete the stitching.

5. Bring the folded edge of the binding to the back and hand stitch it as instructed in step 6 of the French-fold method on page 22. The raw end of the strip will be encased within the binding.

   Note: When hand stitching the bindings for my quilts, I always stitch the miters at each corner to ensure they are secure and to eliminate any gaps.

Making a Hanging Sleeve

A hanging sleeve provides the most efficient way of displaying your quilt on a wall, and it can be made from leftover quilt fabrics or muslin. The following steps will enable you to attach a sleeve as the binding is sewn to the quilt.

1. Cut an 8"-wide strip about 2" shorter than the width of your quilt. Fold the short ends under twice, measuring approximately ¼" with each fold. Machine stitch the folds.

2. Fold the strip in half lengthwise, wrong sides together. Center and baste the folded strip to the back of the quilt, positioning the raw edges flush with the top raw edge of the quilt. As the binding is stitched, the edges of the sleeve will be perma-

nently attached. Use matching thread to blindstitch the bottom of the sleeve to the quilt back.

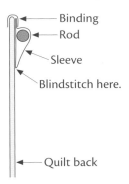

Binding
Rod
Sleeve
Blindstitch here.

Quilt back

Attaching a Quilt Label

Remember to sign and date your quilt using a fabric label, or create your own unique label by adding a muslin border to a small orphan block.

To stabilize the fabric for writing, iron the waxy side of a piece of freezer paper to the wrong side of the fabric. Once you've written the label, peel away the paper, press the raw edges under ¼", and pin the label to the quilt back. Use a small dot of liquid basting glue in the seam allowance at each corner to anchor the label and hand stitch it to the back of the quilt.

Old-Fashioned Hospitality

Create an artful expression of your hospitality with this vividly appliquéd
quilt center, and then frame it to perfection with a vibrant patchwork border.
What better way to convey the warmth of your welcome?

MATERIALS

This colorful project takes much of its charm from the scrappy patchwork blocks used in the quilt center and border. Scraps from approximately 80 different prints were used in the featured quilt, but if your stash isn't that large (yet), fewer prints can be used and repeated throughout the top—just be certain to keep their placement in mind when you cut your patchwork pieces so that your repeated prints don't lie next to each other. When choosing fabrics for the center block, refer to the block illustration on page 28, noting that row 1 is the fabric surrounding the center square.

1⅜ yards of medium green plaid for vines, leaf appliqués, and binding

1 yard of tan print for quilt-center background

¾ yard of cream print for quilt-center background

4 fat eighths (9" x 22") of assorted coordinating prints for rows 1–4 of pieced center block

1 fat quarter (18" x 22") of coordinating print for row 5 of pieced center block (a dark hue works best)

¼ yard (not a fat quarter) of gold print for pineapple appliqués

¼ yard total of 3 assorted green prints for leaf appliqués

1 square, 6" x 6", of black print for berry appliqués

21 squares, 2½" x 2½", of assorted prints for center square of pieced center block and center squares of pieced border blocks

Large scraps, approximately 7" x 7" each, of 20 assorted prints for row 1 of pieced border blocks

Large scraps, approximately 12" x 12" each, of 40 assorted prints for rows 2 and 3 of pieced border blocks and appliqués

4 yards of fabric for backing

67" x 67" square of batting

³⁄₁₆" bias bar

CUTTING

Cut all pieces across the width of the fabric unless otherwise noted. Refer to page 31 for appliqué patterns A–F and to "Invisible Machine Appliqué" beginning on page 10 for pattern piece preparation. For greater ease in piecing the blocks, keep the center and border block pieces separated according to the row number.

From 1 fat eighth of the assorted coordinating prints, cut the following pieces for row 1 of the center block*:
2 squares, 2½" x 2½"
2 rectangles, 2½" x 6½"

From 1 fat eighth of the assorted coordinating prints, cut the following pieces for row 2 of the center block*:
2 rectangles, 1½" x 6½"
2 rectangles, 1½" x 8½"

From 1 fat eighth of the assorted coordinating prints, cut the following pieces for row 3 of the center block*:
2 rectangles, 2½" x 8½"
2 rectangles, 2½" x 12½"

Finished quilt: 60½" x 60½" ■ Finished center: 40" x 40" ■ Finished border blocks: 10" x 10"

Designed, pieced, and machine appliquéd by Kim Diehl. Machine quilted by Celeste Freiberg.

From 1 fat eighth of the assorted coordinating prints, cut the following pieces for row 4 of the center block*:

2 rectangles, 1½" x 12½"

2 rectangles, 1½" x 14½"

From the fat quarter of coordinating print, cut the following pieces for row 5 of the center block*:

2 rectangles, 3½" x 14½"

2 rectangles, 3½" x 20½"

From the tan print, cut:

8 squares, 10½" x 10½"

From the cream print, cut:

4 rectangles, 10½" x 20½"

From the gold print, cut:

4 using pattern A

From the medium green plaid, cut:

7 strips, 2½" x 42" (binding)

From the bias of the remaining medium green plaid, cut:

8 strips, 1" x 26"

4 using pattern B

From the 3 assorted green prints and the scraps of the medium green plaid, cut a combined total of:

12 using pattern C

12 using pattern C reversed

56 using pattern E

PIN POINT

Easily Achieving a Folk-Art Look

It's easy to achieve the look and feel of folk art for any appliqué quilt. As you cut out your appliqué pattern pieces, simply wiggle your scissors slightly as you cut along the traced lines of your shapes. This little trick will transform even the most traditional design into a project with the primitive look of folk art.

From the 6" x 6" square of black print, cut:

12 using pattern F

From each of the 7" x 7" scraps of 20 assorted prints, cut the following pieces for row 1 of the border blocks*:

2 rectangles, 1½" x 2½" (combined total of 40)

2 rectangles, 1½" x 4½" (combined total of 40)

From each of 20 of the 12" x 12" scraps of assorted prints, cut the following pieces for row 2 of the border blocks*:

2 rectangles, 2½" x 4½" (combined total of 40)

2 rectangles, 2½" x 8½" (combined total of 40)

From each of the remaining 12" x 12" scraps of assorted prints, cut the following pieces for row 3 of the border blocks*:

2 rectangles, 1½" x 8½" (combined total of 40)

2 rectangles, 1½" x 10½" (combined total of 40)

From the remainder of the 12" x 12" scraps used for the pieced border blocks, cut:

8 using pattern D

*Refer to the quilt photo on page 26 as you make your fabric choices for the border blocks.

PIECING THE CENTER BLOCK

Sew all pieces with right sides together unless otherwise noted.

1. Join two matching print 2½" squares cut for row 1 of the center block to opposite sides of one assorted print 2½" center square to form a pieced rectangle. Press the seam allowances away from the center square. Join a matching print 2½" x 6½" rectangle to each long side of the pieced rectangle. Press the seam allowances away from the pieced rectangle.

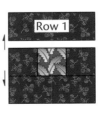

2. Continue joining and pressing the rectangles for rows 2 through 5 to the step 1 unit in numerical order, always joining the shortest rectangles for each new row to the seamed sides of the block first, and then following with the longer rectangles. Press all seam allowances away from the block center. The pieced block should now measure 20½" square, including the seam allowances.

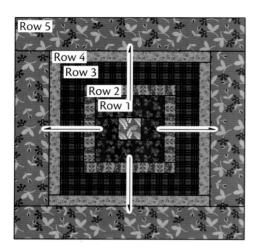

3. Lightly draw a diagonal line on the wrong side of four of the tan print 10½" squares. Position a square on two opposite corners of the pieced center unit as shown. Stitch the squares to the unit exactly on the drawn lines. Fold the resulting triangle open, aligning the raw edges with the pieced block underneath to keep it square. Trim away the excess layers of fabric underneath the top triangle, leaving a ¼" seam allowance. Repeat with the remaining corners of the unit to complete the block.

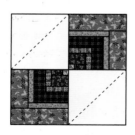
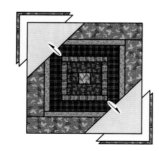

PIECING THE QUILT CENTER

1. Join cream print 10½" x 20½" rectangles to the right and left sides of the pieced center block. Press the seam allowances toward the cream print.

2. Join a tan print 10½" square to each end of the two remaining cream print 10½" x 20½" rectangles to make a pieced rectangle. Press the seam allowances toward the cream print. Join a pieced rectangle to each remaining side of the center block. Press the seam allowances toward the cream print. The pieced center unit should now measure 40½" square, including the seam allowances.

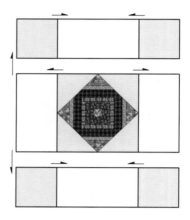

APPLIQUÉING THE QUILT CENTER

1. Carefully fold the center unit in half diagonally and lightly press a crease from the center square out to each opposite corner. Repeat with the remaining corners.

2. Referring to "Making Bias-Tube Stems and Vines" on page 13, prepare the medium green plaid 1" x 26" strips.

3. With right sides together, carefully fold a prepared A appliqué in half vertically and lightly finger-press a center crease. Referring to the quilt photo, position the appliqué onto the quilt background, aligning the appliqué crease with the background crease to center it and positioning the bottom edge approximately 1" up from the pieced center block. Pin or baste the bottom portion of the appliqué in place, leaving the top edge free for adding the C appliqués.

4. Referring to the quilt photo, position one prepared B appliqué at the top of the pineapple, aligning the top point with the background crease to center it; tuck the bottom raw edge under the pineapple at least ¼"; pin or baste in place. Position and baste three C and three C reversed appliqués on each side of the center B appliqué to form the pineapple top; ensure that all raw ends are tucked under the pineapple at least ¼".

5. Fold back the top portion of the A appliqué and anchor it in place with a pin. Referring to "Stitching the Appliqués" on page 15, stitch the B and C appliqués to the background. Remove the paper pattern pieces as instructed in "Removing Paper Pattern Pieces" on page 16. Reposition the top edge of A and appliqué it in place. Remove the paper pattern piece.

6. Referring to the quilt photo, position, baste, and stitch D appliqués to the background on each side of the pineapple. Remove the paper pattern pieces.

7. Beginning at one raw end of a prepared vine and working out toward the opposite end, apply tiny dots of liquid basting glue along the seam allowance. Press the vine onto the quilt top starting at the center background crease and positioning it so the vine rests against the bottom edge of the pineapple. Curve the vine out toward each D appliqué, swirling it around and onto the stitched circles. Trim away any unnecessary length to achieve the look you desire. Repeat with a second vine, again positioning one raw end at the center background crease to butt the raw edges together and swirling the vine outward to loosely form a mirror image of the first vine.

8. Using the quilt photo as a guide, lay out and baste twelve E appliqués along the vine, with six leaves positioned on each side of the pineapple. Lay out and baste two more E appliqués on the lower edge of the pineapple, with the bottom tips resting just to each side of the raw vine ends at the pineapple center. Appliqué the vines and leaves in place and remove the paper pattern pieces.

9. Referring to the quilt photo, position, baste, and stitch three F appliqués to the quilt top, ensuring that the appliqué placed on the pineapple covers the raw vine ends.

Appliqué placement diagram

10. Repeat steps 3–9 to complete the appliqué on each side of the pieced center block.

PIECING AND ADDING THE BORDERS

1. Referring to step 1 of "Piecing the Center Block" on page 27, select an assorted print 2½" center square and a matching set of four rectangles cut for row 1 of the border blocks. Join a 1½" x 2½" rectangle to opposite sides of the 2½" square to form a pieced rectangle. Press the seam allowances away from the center square. Join a matching print 1½" x 4½" rectangle to each long side of the pieced rectangle. Press the seam allowances away from the pieced rectangle.

2. Continue joining and pressing the rectangles for rows 2 and 3 as instructed in step 2 of "Piecing the Center Block" on page 28. Remember to join the shortest rectangles for each new row to the seamed sides of the block first, and then follow with the longer rectangles. Press all seam allowances away from the block center.

3. Repeat steps 1 and 2 for a total of 20 border blocks measuring 10½" square, including the seam allowances.

4. Join four border blocks to make a pieced strip. Press the seam allowances in one direction. Repeat to make a second pieced strip. Join these strips to the right and left sides of the quilt center. Carefully press the seam allowances away from the quilt center, taking care not to apply heat to the appliqués.

5. Join and press six border blocks as instructed in step 4. Repeat to make a total of two pieced border strips.

Make 2.

6. Join the pieced strips from step 5 to the remaining sides of the quilt center. Carefully press the seam allowances away from the quilt center. The pieced and appliquéd quilt top should now measure 60½" square, including the seam allowances.

COMPLETING THE QUILT

Refer to "Finishing Techniques" on page 19 for details as needed. Layer the quilt top, batting, and backing. Quilt the layers. The featured quilt was machine quilted with a stylized feathered wreath in the center block. The surrounding background areas were quilted with a pebbled design on the cream print and the tan areas were "McTavished" (free-form outlines that are echo quilted inward, a technique developed by professional long-arm quilter Karen McTavish). The pineapples were stippled with randomly placed asterisks to add texture, and a serpentine wave of feathers was quilted onto the border blocks. Join the seven medium green plaid 2½" x 42" strips into one length and use it to bind the quilt.

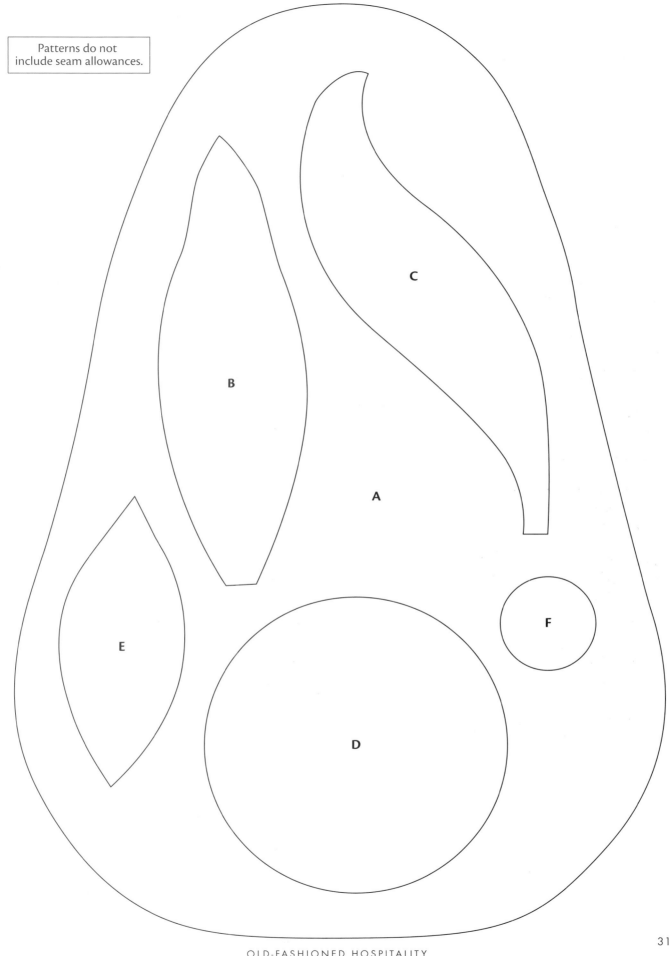

Patterns do not include seam allowances.

B

C

A

F

E

D

All in a Row

Combine traditional blocks with a fresh approach to color and what is the happy result? A charming yet modern quilt, where old suddenly becomes new again.

MATERIALS

50 "chubby sixteenths" (9" x 11") *or* 3⅝ yards *total* of assorted prints for blocks

25 squares, 6" x 6", or ⅞ yard *total* of assorted prints for nine-patch units

⅞ yard of brown print for sashing squares, border corners, and binding

¾ yard of neutral print for sashing strips

¾ yard of dark orange print for border

3¼ yards of fabric for backing

58" x 58" square of batting

CUTTING

Cut all pieces across the width of the fabric unless otherwise noted.

From *each* of the 25 assorted print 6" x 6" squares, cut:

9 squares, 1½" x 1½" (combined total of 225)

From *each* of the 50 assorted print chubby sixteenths, cut*:

2 squares, 2⅞" x 2⅞" (combined total of 100); cut each square once diagonally to yield 4 triangles

4 rectangles, 1½" x 3½" (combined total of 200)

For greater ease in piecing the blocks, keep the patchwork sets organized by print.

From the neutral print, cut:

14 strips, 1½" x 42"; crosscut into:
    60 rectangles, 1½" x 7½"
    8 rectangles, 1½" x 5½"

From the brown print, cut:

2 strips, 1½" x 42"; crosscut into 36 squares, 1½" x 1½"

1 strip, 5½" x 42"; crosscut into 4 squares, 5½" x 5½"

6 strips, 2½" x 42" (binding)

From the dark orange print, cut:

4 strips, 5½" x 39½"

Finished quilt: 51½" x 51½" ■ Finished blocks: 7" x 7"
Designed by Kim Diehl. Pieced by Deb Behrend. Machine quilted by Celeste Freiberg.

PIECING THE CHURN DASH VARIATION BLOCKS

Sew all pieces with right sides together unless otherwise noted.

1. Select four matching 1½" squares cut from one assorted print 6" square and five matching 1½" squares cut from a second assorted print 6" square. Set aside the remaining squares from each print for use when piecing the remaining nine-patch units.

PIN POINT

Mixing Your Patchwork Prints

I've found that the secret to successfully mixing many different prints is to noticeably vary the size and scale of the patterns that are placed next to each other. Whenever possible, I place larger and smaller prints together, rather than positioning those of the same scale side by side. If I find that many of my prints are of a similar size, I'll vary the value of the colors to achieve contrast and add further definition. When my goal is to achieve a finished quilt with a bit of the "make do" look, I toss these guidelines out the window and embrace the less-than-perfect combinations that sometimes result.

2. Lay out the squares as shown to form a nine-patch unit. Join the squares in each horizontal row. Press the seam allowances of each row in alternating directions. Join the rows. Press the seam allowances in one direction.

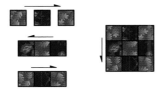

3. Repeat steps 1 and 2 for a total of 25 nine-patch units sewn from assorted pairs of prints, with each unit measuring 3½" square, including the seam allowances.

4. Select a set of patchwork pieces cut from two assorted print chubby sixteenths (it isn't necessary that one set be light and one set be dark, only that the two prints are contrasting).

5. Join a 2⅞" triangle from each print along the long bias edges. Press the seam allowance to one side. Trim away the dog-ear points. Repeat for a total of four half-square-triangle units.

Make 4 from
each pair of prints.

6. Join one 1½" x 3½" rectangle from each print as shown. Press the seam allowance to one side. Repeat for a total of four pieced rectangle units.

Make 4 from
each pair of prints.

7. Lay out one nine-patch unit from step 2, four half-square-triangle units from step 5, and four pieced rectangles from step 6 as shown. Join the units in each horizontal row. Press the seam allowances toward the pieced rectangle units. Join the rows. Press the seam allowances toward the middle row.

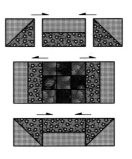 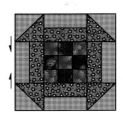

8. Repeat steps 4–7 for a total of 25 Churn Dash Variation blocks measuring 7½" square, including the seam allowances.

PIECING THE QUILT CENTER

1. Lay out six brown print 1½" squares and five neutral print 1½" x 7½" rectangles in alternating positions. Join the pieces. Press the seam allowances toward the neutral print. Repeat for a total of six sashing rows.

Make 6.

2. Lay out six neutral print 1½" x 7½" rectangles and five Churn Dash Variation blocks in a row as shown. Press the seam allowances toward the neutral print. Repeat for a total of five block rows.

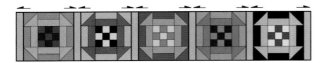

Make 5.

3. Lay out six sashing rows and five block rows as shown. Join the rows. Press the seam allowances toward the sashing rows. The pieced quilt center should now measure 41½" square, including the seam allowances.

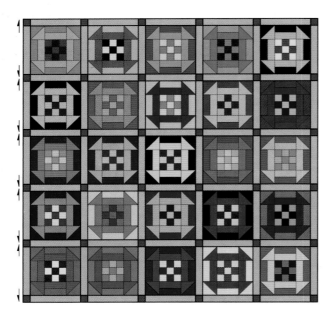

PIECING AND ADDING THE BORDERS

1. Join a neutral print 1½" x 5½" rectangle to each end of a dark orange print 5½" x 39½" strip. Press the seam allowance toward the neutral print. Repeat for a total of two pieced border strips. Join these strips to the right and left sides of the quilt center. Press the seam allowances toward the orange border strips.

Make 2.

2. Lay out two brown print 5½" squares, two neutral print 1½" x 5½" rectangles, and one orange print 5½" x 39½" strip as shown. Join the pieces. Press the seam allowances toward the neutral print. Repeat for a total of two pieced border rows. Join these rows to the remaining sides of the quilt center. Press the seam allowances toward the

orange border rows. The pieced quilt top should measure 51½" square, including the seam allowances.

Make 2.

COMPLETING THE QUILT

Refer to "Finishing Techniques" on page 19 for details as needed. Layer the quilt top, batting, and backing. Quilt the layers. The blocks of the featured quilt were machine quilted with a squared feathered wreath radiating out from the seams of the center nine-patch units, and Xs were stitched onto the nine-patch centers. The sashing strips were quilted with a cable design, and the brown corner post squares were quilted with Xs. Serpentine feathered vines were quilted in the borders, and feathered Xs were quilted onto the border corner squares. Join the six brown print 2½" x 42" strips into one length and use it to bind the quilt.

PIN POINT

Portable Organization

To easily organize patchwork sets or appliqué pieces, especially for travel or classes, try layering them between paper plates. Special notes or instructions can be written directly on each plate, and the plates can be stacked together to keep your work neat, compact, and easily portable.

Bloomin' Wonderful

Bring the informal beauty of a country garden indoors with these budding trumpet blooms and velvety-soft leaves of mossy green. Modest but so appealing, these blossoms could never be mistaken for wallflowers.

MATERIALS

1⅝ yards of medium tan print 1 for border

1½ yards of dark tan print for sashing, border corner posts, and binding

1¼ yards of medium green print for stem and leaf appliqués

9 fat eighths (9" x 22") of assorted medium and dark prints for bloom and block-center appliqués

1 yard of light tan print for block backgrounds

1 yard of medium tan print 2 for block backgrounds

1 fat quarter of brown print for sashing corner posts

4 yards of fabric for backing

71" x 71" square of batting

CUTTING

Cut all strips across the width of the fabric unless otherwise noted. Refer to page 43 for appliqué patterns A–F and to "Invisible Machine Appliqué" beginning on page 10 for pattern piece preparation.

From the light tan print, cut:
18 squares, 7½" x 7½"

From medium tan print 2 for block backgrounds, cut:
18 squares, 7½" x 7½"

From each of the 9 assorted fat eighths, cut:
1 using pattern A (combined total of 9)

4 using pattern B (combined total of 36). For added interest, cut some of the pieces using the reversed B pattern.

1 using pattern F (combined total of 9)

From the medium green print, cut:
9 using pattern C

72 using pattern D

72 using pattern E

From the dark tan print, cut:
12 strips, 2½" x 42"; crosscut into 24 strips, 2½" x 14½". Reserve the scraps from these strips for use as binding.

1 strip, 7½" x 42"; crosscut into 4 squares, 7½" x 7½"

Enough 2½"-wide strips to make a 266" length of binding when joined end to end with the reserved strips from above

From the brown print fat quarter, cut:
16 squares, 2½" x 2½"

From the lengthwise grain of medium tan print 1 for border, cut:
4 strips, 7½" x 50½"

Finished quilt: 64½" x 64½" ■ Finished blocks: 14" x 14"
Designed, pieced, and machine appliquéd by Kim Diehl. Machine quilted by Cynthia Fuelling.

PIN POINT

Recycling Your Appliqué Scraps

To make the most of the scraps that remain after cutting away the backs of your larger appliqués, press them flat (if needed), and reuse them to prepare smaller appliqués. For this project, the scraps from your trimmed A appliqués can be recycled and used for the F appliqués. No waste!

PIECING THE BLOCKS

Sew all pieces with right sides together unless otherwise noted.

1. Join a medium tan print 2 and a light tan print 7½" square. Press the seam allowance toward the medium tan print. Repeat to make a total of 18 pieced rectangles.

2. Join two pieced rectangles to form a four-patch unit. Press the seam allowances to one side. Repeat for a total of nine pieced block backgrounds measuring 14½" square, including the seam allowances.

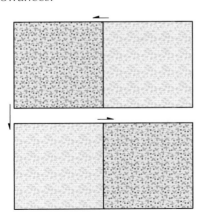

Make 9.

APPLIQUÉING THE BLOCKS

1. Select a matching set of prepared A, B, and F appliqués. With right sides together, fold and finger-press a horizontal center crease in the A appliqué. Unfold and repeat to form a vertical center crease.

2. Line up the creases of the A appliqué with the seams of a pieced block background to center it; pin or baste in place. Referring to "Stitching the Appliqués" on page 15, stitch the appliqué to the background. Referring to "Removing Paper Pattern Pieces" on page 16, remove the paper pattern piece.

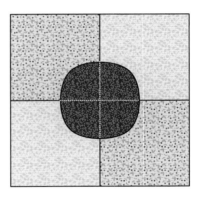

3. Fold a C appliqué into fourths to create creases in the same positions as on the paper pattern piece. Unfold and center the C appliqué over the stitched A appliqué, lining up the creases with the block seams to center it. Baste or pin the appliqué in place, leaving the stem tips unpinned. Using the quilt photo as a guide, position a B appliqué under each stem tip, overlapping the pieces by at least ¼". Pin or baste the B appliqués in place. Fold the stem tips back from the B appliqués and secure them with pins. Stitch the B appliqués and remove the paper pattern pieces. Reposition and baste the stem tips; stitch the C appliqué in place. Remove the paper pattern piece.

4. Referring to the quilt photo, position, baste, and stitch eight D appliqués, eight E appliqués, and one F appliqué. Remove the paper pattern pieces. If necessary, lightly and briefly press the block from the back.

5. Repeat steps 1–4 for a total of nine appliquéd blocks.

PIECING THE QUILT CENTER

1. Lay out four brown print 2½" squares and three dark tan print 2½" x 14½" strips in alternating positions. Join the pieces. Press the seam allowances toward the dark tan print. Repeat for a total of four pieced sashing rows.

Make 4.

2. Lay out four dark tan 2½" x 14½" strips and three appliquéd blocks as shown. Join the pieces. Carefully press the seam allowances toward the dark tan sashing strips, taking care not to apply heat to the appliqués. Repeat for a total of three block rows.

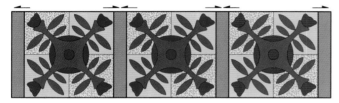

Make 3.

3. Using the quilt photo as a guide, lay out four sashing rows and three block rows. Join the rows. Carefully press the seam allowances toward the sashing rows. The pieced quilt center should now measure 50½" square, including the seam allowances.

PIECING AND ADDING THE BORDERS

1. Join a 7½" x 50½" medium tan print 1 border strip to the right and left sides of the quilt center. Press the seam allowances toward the quilt center.

2. Join a dark tan print 7½" square to each end of the remaining two border strips. Press the seam allowances toward the dark tan squares. Join these pieced strips to the remaining sides of the quilt center. Press the seam allowances toward the quilt center. The pieced quilt top should measure 64½" square, including the seam allowances.

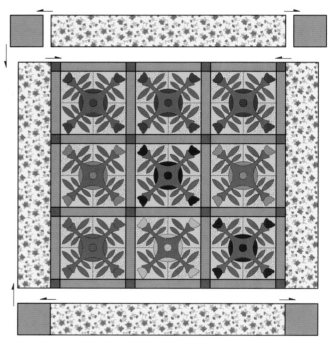

COMPLETING THE QUILT

Refer to "Finishing Techniques" on page 19 for details as needed. Layer the quilt top, batting, and backing. Quilt the layers. The light tan block-background areas of the featured quilt were quilted with a McTavishing design and the medium tan areas with a small stipple design to emphasize the four-patch units. Stylized stitched accents were placed onto the appliqués of each block, Xs were quilted onto the corner posts, and feathered motifs were stitched onto the sashing strips and borders. Join the 2½"-wide dark tan print lengths to form a 266" length of binding and use it to bind the quilt.

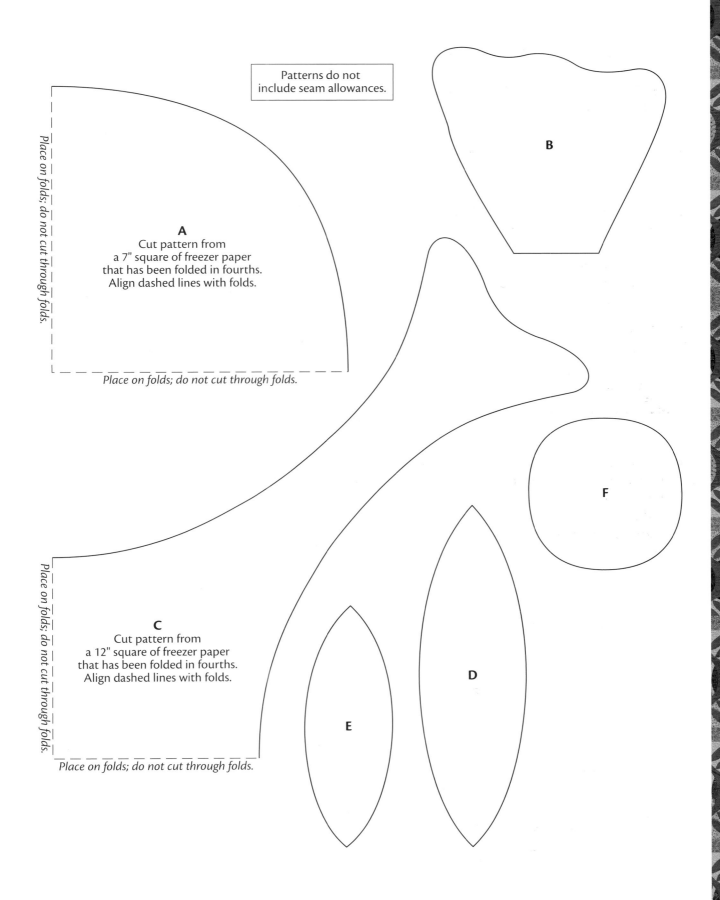

Patterns do not
include seam allowances.

B

Place on folds; do not cut through folds.

A
Cut pattern from
a 7" square of freezer paper
that has been folded in fourths.
Align dashed lines with folds.

Place on folds; do not cut through folds.

F

Place on folds; do not cut through folds.

C
Cut pattern from
a 12" square of freezer paper
that has been folded in fourths.
Align dashed lines with folds.

D

E

Place on folds; do not cut through folds.

Cabin Cozy

Embrace your frugal nature and use the tiniest saved scraps of your favorite prints in this quilt with classic appeal. Best of all, clever placement of your neutrals provides an unexpected and pleasing secondary design, letting your scrappy blocks shine.

MATERIALS

1½ yards *total* of assorted tan prints for blocks and sashing

1½ yards *total* of assorted cream prints for blocks and sashing

1⅓ yards of cranberry print for sashing strip corner posts and border

1¼ yards *total* of assorted prints for blocks and binding

⅓ yard of dark tan print for border

1 fat quarter (18" x 22") of cream print for border corner blocks

3½ yards of fabric for backing

64" x 64" square of batting

CUTTING

Cut all pieces across the width of the fabric unless otherwise noted.

From the assorted tan prints, cut a *combined total* of:

36 squares, 1⅞" x 1⅞"; cut each square once diagonally to yield 72 triangles

18 squares, 1½" x 1½"

18 rectangles, 1½" x 3½"

36 rectangles, 1½" x 4½"

36 rectangles, 1½" x 5½"

62 rectangles, 1½" x 6½"

From the assorted cream prints, cut a *combined total* of:

36 squares, 1⅞" x 1⅞"; cut each square once diagonally to yield 72 triangles

18 squares, 1½" x 1½"

18 rectangles, 1½" x 3½"

36 rectangles, 1½" x 4½"

36 rectangles, 1½" x 5½"

58 rectangles, 1½" x 6½"

From the assorted prints, cut a *combined total* of:

104 squares, 1⅞" x 1⅞"; cut each square once diagonally to yield 208 triangles

52 squares, 2½" x 2½"

Enough 2½"-wide random lengths to make a 238" length of binding when joined end to end

From the fat quarter of cream print, cut:

32 squares, 1⅞" x 1⅞"; cut each square once diagonally to yield 64 triangles

16 squares, 1½" x 1½"

From the *lengthwise grain* of the cranberry print, cut:

8 strips, 3½" x 43½"

From the remaining cranberry print, cut:

53 squares, 1½" x 1½"

From the dark tan print, cut:

6 strips, 1½" x 42"; crosscut 1 strip into 8 rectangles, 1½" x 3½"

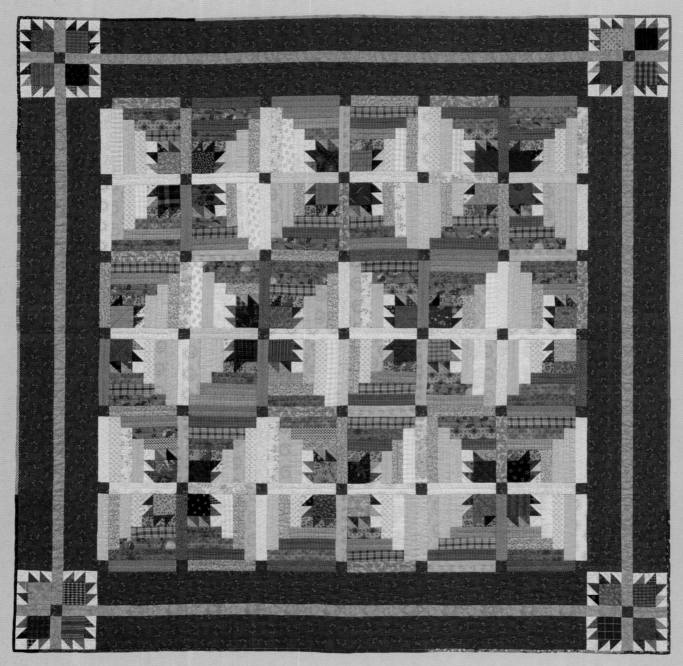

Finished quilt: 57½" x 57½" ■ Finished blocks: 6" x 6"
Designed, pieced, and hand quilted by Kim Diehl.

PIECING THE HALF-SQUARE-TRIANGLE UNITS

Sew all pieces with right sides together unless otherwise noted.

1. Join an assorted print 1⅞" triangle and an assorted tan print 1⅞" triangle along the long bias edges. Press the seam allowance toward the assorted print. Trim away the dog-ear points. Repeat for a total of 72 tan print half-square-triangle units.

Make 72.

2. Repeat step 1 using the assorted print 1⅞" triangles and assorted cream print 1⅞" triangles to make a total of 72 assorted cream print half-square-triangle units.

3. Repeat step 1 using the assorted print 1⅞" triangles and cream print 1⅞" triangles to make a total of 64 cream print half-square-triangle units.

PIECING THE BEAR'S PAW A UNITS

1. Lay out two tan print half-square-triangle units and one assorted tan print 1½" square. Join the pieces. Press the seam allowances toward the tan print square. Repeat for a total of 18 tan print pieced rectangles.

Make 18.

2. Join two assorted cream print half-square-triangle units. Press the seam allowances toward the assorted print. Join this rectangle unit to an assorted print 2½" square. Press the seam allowances toward the assorted print square. Repeat for a total of 18 assorted cream print units.

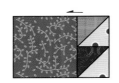

Make 18.

3. Join a tan print pieced rectangle from step 1 to a cream print unit from step 2. Press the seam allowance toward the cream print unit. Repeat for a total of 18 bear's paw A units measuring 3½" square, including the seam allowances.

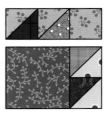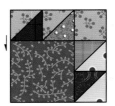

Unit A.
Make 18.

PIECING THE BEAR'S PAW B UNITS

1. Lay out two assorted cream print half-square-triangle units and one assorted cream print 1½" square. Join the pieces. Press the seam allowances toward the cream print square. Repeat for a total of 18 assorted cream print pieced rectangles.

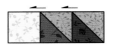

Make 18.

2. Join two tan print half-square-triangle units. Press the seam allowances toward the assorted print. Join this rectangle unit to an assorted print 2½" square. Press the seam allowances toward the assorted print square. Repeat for a total of 18 tan print units.

Make 18.

3. Join a cream print pieced rectangle from step 1 to a tan print unit from step 2 as shown. Press the seam allowance toward the tan print unit. Repeat for a total of 18 bear's paw B units measuring 3½" square, including the seam allowances.

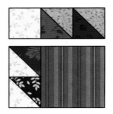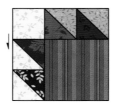

Unit B.
Make 18.

PIECING THE A AND B BLOCKS

1. Lay out an A unit and the assorted tan and assorted cream pieces in order as shown. Join the assorted cream print 3½"-long strip to the A unit. Press the seam allowance toward the cream print strip. Join and press the assorted tan print 4½"-long strip to the unit in the same manner. Continue joining and pressing the cream and tan print strips in the order shown. Repeat for a total of 18 Bear's Paw A blocks measuring 6½" square, including the seam allowances.

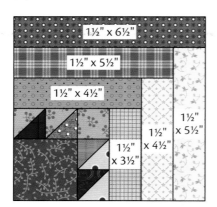

Block A.
Make 18.

PIN POINT

Achieving a Perfectly Sized Block

If you find that your pieced blocks are consistently just a skosh small, even when using a quarter-inch foot, here's a quick little trick that may make a difference in your accuracy. For sewing machines with incremental needle positions, try setting the needle just one notch to the right of the center position. Sew a test block and measure your results—this slight adjustment can be just enough to compensate for the thread or two that is lost to the fold of fabric when your seam allowances are pressed.

2. Lay out a B unit and the assorted tan and assorted cream strips as shown. Sew and press the block in order in the same manner as for the A block. Repeat for a total of 18 Bear's Paw B blocks measuring 6½" square, including the seam allowances.

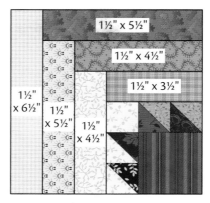

Block B.
Make 18.

PIECING THE ROWS

1. Lay out seven cranberry print 1½" squares and six assorted tan print 1½" x 6½" strips. Join the pieces. Press the seam allowances toward the tan print strips. Repeat for a total of four tan sashing rows.

Make 4.

2. Lay out seven cranberry print 1½" squares and six assorted cream print 1½" x 6½" strips. Join the pieces. Press the seam allowances toward the cream print strips. Repeat for a total of three cream print sashing rows.

Make 3.

3. Lay out three B blocks, three A blocks, four assorted cream print 1½" x 6½" strips, and three assorted tan print 1½" x 6½" strips as shown. Join the pieces. Press the seam allowances toward the sashing strips. Repeat for a total of four A block rows.

Block A row.
Make 4.

4. Lay out three A blocks, three B blocks, four assorted tan print 1½" x 6½" strips, and three assorted cream print 1½" x 6½" strips as shown. Sew and press the pieces as instructed in step 3. Repeat for a total of two B block rows.

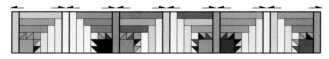

Block B row.
Make 2.

PIECING THE QUILT CENTER

Referring to the illustration, lay out the sashing rows and block rows to form the quilt center. Join the rows. Press the seam allowances toward the sashing rows.

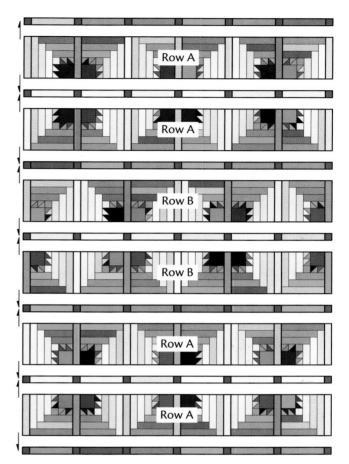

PIECING AND ADDING THE BORDERS

1. Referring to steps 1–3 of "Piecing the Bear's Paw A Units" on page 47, use four cream print half-square-triangle units, one cream print 1½" square, and one assorted print 2½" square to make a bear's-paw unit. Repeat for a total of 16 bear's-paw border units measuring 3½" square, including the seam allowances.

2. Cut and piece the dark tan print 1½" x 42" strips to make four border strips measuring 1½" x 49½". Press the seam allowances to one side.

3. Referring to the border assembly illustration, sew a cranberry print 3½" x 43½" strip to the top and bottom edges of the quilt center. Press the seam allowances toward the cranberry print. Sew a bear's-paw border unit from step 1 to each end of a cranberry print 3½" x 43½" strip as shown. Repeat for a total of two strips. Join these strips to the right and left sides of the quilt center. Press the seam allowances toward the cranberry strips.

4. Join a dark tan print 1½" x 49½" strip to the top and bottom edges of the quilt top. Press the seam allowances toward the tan strips. Join a cranberry print 1½" square to each end of the remaining 49½"-long strips. Press the seam allowances toward the tan print. Join these pieced strips to the right and left sides of the quilt top. Press the seam allowances toward the tan strips.

5. Lay out and join two dark tan print 1½" x 3½" rectangles, two bear's-paw border units from step 1, and one cranberry print 3½" x 43½" strip as shown. Press the seam allowances away from the bear's-paw units. Repeat for a total of four pieced strips. Join two of these strips to the top and bottom edges of the quilt top. Press the seam allowances toward the cranberry strips. Join a bear's-paw border unit from step 1 to each end of the remaining pieced strips. Press the seam allowances away from the bear's-paw units. Join these strips to the remaining sides of the quilt top. Press the seam allowances toward the cranberry strips. The pieced quilt top should now measure 57½" square, including the seam allowances.

COMPLETING THE QUILT

Refer to "Finishing Techniques" on page 19 for details as needed. Lay out the quilt top, batting, and backing. Quilt the layers. The bear's-paw units of the featured quilt were hand quilted with Xs stitched onto the assorted print 2½" squares and the half-square-triangle units were outlined in the neutral areas ¼" outside of the seam lines. The cream and tan print block strips were quilted with straight lines running through the center of the strips. The cranberry print borders were quilted with a series of straight lines placed at consistently repeating intervals and a running cable was stitched over the center dark tan sashing strips. Join the 2½"-wide random lengths of assorted prints into one length and use it to bind the quilt.

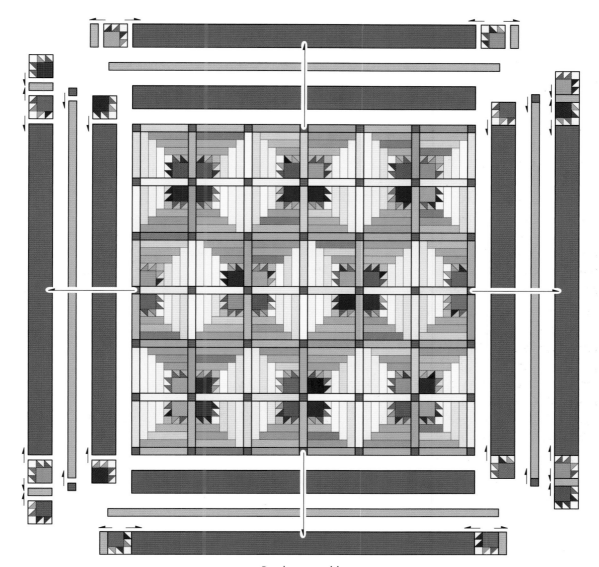

Border assembly

Serendipity Sampler

Toss tradition to the wind, add a dollop of whimsy, and let the flowers fall where they may in this happy and exuberant quilt that's sure to tickle your fancy!

MATERIALS

You can easily give this quilt a more traditional feel by substituting an assortment of neutral prints for the quilt center and using an assortment of light and medium prints, rather than plaid and striped fabrics, for the border.

3⅛ yards *total* of assorted light to medium plaid and striped fabrics for block backgrounds

3 yards *total* of assorted print scraps for appliqués. The featured quilt uses a variety of deep red, green, and blue prints for the flowers, leaves, and berries and an assortment of different prints for the flower centers.

2 yards *total* of assorted medium to dark plaid and striped fabrics for outer border

1⅛ yards *total* of assorted red prints for inner border and binding

⅝ yard of dark green print for stems and vines

4½ yards of fabric for backing

73" x 82" piece of batting

½" bias bar

CUTTING

Cut all pieces across the width of the fabric unless otherwise noted.

From the assorted light to medium plaid and striped fabrics, cut:
119 rectangles, 3½" x 6½"

102 squares, 3½" x 3½"

From the assorted medium to dark plaid and striped fabrics, cut:
78 rectangles, 3½" x 6½"

4 squares, 6⅞" x 6⅞"; cut each square once diagonally to yield 8 triangles

PIN POINT

Cutting Plaid and Striped Fabrics

When cutting patchwork pieces from plaid and striped fabrics, particularly when they are woven rather than printed, I recommend cutting them from a single layer of cloth rather than from multiple thicknesses. Align a stripe or straight line from the design of the plaid with the marked lines on your cutting mat to ensure the design is not running at an angle and make your cuts. If the weave of the cloth isn't perfectly straight, I suggest choosing the most dominant line of the pattern as your starting point. The extra moment this step takes will really enhance your project with patchwork lines that run straight and true.

From the *bias* of the dark green print, cut:
Enough 2"-wide lengths to make a 196" length when joined end to end using straight seams

From the assorted red prints, cut:
Enough 2"-wide random lengths to make a 240" length when joined end to end using straight seams

Enough 2½"-wide random lengths to make a 300" length of binding when joined end to end

Finished quilt: 66½" x 75½" ■ Finished blocks: 24" x 24"

Designed, pieced, and machine appliquéd by Kim Diehl. Machine quilted by Celeste Freiberg.

CUTTING AND PREPARING THE APPLIQUÉS

1. Referring to "Making Bias-Tube Stems and Vines" on page 13, prepare the dark green 196" bias strip.

2. Refer to pages 59–65 for the appliqué patterns and to "Invisible Machine Appliqué" beginning on page 10 for pattern piece preparation. Cut the pieces from the assorted print scraps, referring to the quilt photo if necessary as you make your fabric choices. For ease of preparation, the appliqué requirements are provided separately for each individual block. Also, use the wreath guide pattern on page 61 to cut one guide from freezer paper.

BLOCK 1	
Pattern	**Amount to cut**
A, B, C	1 *each*
D, E, F	4 *each*
Medium leaf	8
Berry	24
Prepared vine	Four 6" lengths and four 4½" lengths

BLOCK 2	
Pattern	**Amount to cut**
G, H	4 *each*
I, J, large leaf, small leaf	4 *each*
Medium leaf	16
Berry	24
Prepared vine	One 42" length

BLOCK 3	
Pattern	**Amount to cut**
K, L, M, N	4 *each*
O	8
P, Q	1 *each*
Large leaf, small leaf	2
Medium leaf	6
Berry	15
Prepared vine	One 28" length, two 3½" lengths, and four 2½" lengths

BLOCK 4	
Pattern	Amount to cut
R, S, T, U	1 *each*
V, W, X	4 *each*
Medium leaf	8
Berry	20
Prepared vine	Four 7½" lengths

BLOCK 5	
Pattern	Amount to Cut
Y, Z, AA	1 *each*
BB	4
Medium leaf	20
Berry	12
Prepared vine	Two 9" lengths and two 6" lengths

PIECING THE BLOCKS AND SASHING STRIPS

Sew all pieces with right sides together unless otherwise noted.

1. Lay out 24 assorted light to medium plaid 3½" x 6½" rectangles and 16 assorted light to medium plaid 3½" squares in five alternating rows of eight pieces each. Join the pieces in each row.

Press the seam allowances of each row in alternating directions. Join the rows. Press the seam allowances toward the rows of squares. Repeat for a total of four pieced block backgrounds measuring 24½" square, including the seam allowances.

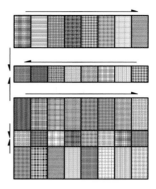

Make 4.

2. Lay out 17 light to medium plaid 3½" x 6½" rectangles and 34 light to medium plaid 3½" squares in three alternating rows of 17 pieces each. Join the pieces in each row. Press the seam allowances of each row in alternating directions. Join the rows. Press the seam allowances toward the rows of squares. The pieced block 5 background unit should measure 12½" x 51½", including the seam allowances.

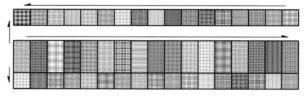

Make 1.

3. Join three light to medium plaid 3½" x 6½" rectangles and two light to medium plaid 3½" squares as shown to make a sashing strip. Press the seam allowances toward the squares. Repeat for a total of two pieced sashing strips.

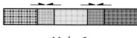

Make 2.

APPLIQUÉING THE BLOCKS

1. With right sides together, fold each pieced 24" square block background in half horizontally. Lightly press a crease through the center row of rectangles. In the same manner, press horizontal and vertical creases through the center row of rectangles in the block 5 background unit.

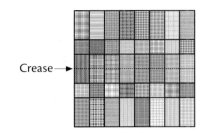

Crease →

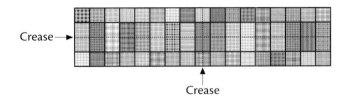

Crease →

Crease

2. For block 1, fold the prepared A circle appliqué in half vertically and lightly finger-press a center crease. Refold horizontally and lightly press a second crease. Unfold the appliqué and center it on the block background, aligning the creases with the block center seam and horizontal crease. Referring to the quilt photo, tuck four prepared 6" stems and four 4½" stems under the A circle approximately ¼". Pin or baste the stems to the background so they curve in one direction. Remove the A appliqué. Referring to "Stitching the Appliqués" on page 15, stitch the stems in place. Reposition, baste, and stitch the A appliqué. Referring to "Removing Paper Pattern Pieces" on page 16, remove the pattern piece. Working from the bottom layer to the top, continue positioning, basting, and stitching the remaining appliqués. Remember to remove the paper pattern pieces before adding each new layer.

3. For block 2, use the pattern creases to center the freezer-paper wreath guide, shiny side down, on a block foundation. Use a hot, dry iron to fuse it in place. Pin or baste the prepared 42" length of vine around the edge of the fused paper circle. Turn the raw ends of the vine under ¼" where they meet

and anchor them in place with liquid glue, trimming any necessary length so that they butt together. Remove the circle template. Referring to the quilt photo, tuck four G stems and four H stems under the basted vine, overlapping the raw ends well so they'll be hidden; baste in place. Stitch the vine and stems. Working from the bottom layer to the top, continue positioning, basting, and stitching the remaining appliqués.

4. For block 3, use the fold lines to cut away the top quarter of the template as shown. Center and iron the prepared template on a block foundation, with the opening positioned at the top. Referring to step 3, position and baste the prepared 28" length of vine onto the background around the edge of the paper template. Remove the template. Referring to the quilt photo, tuck two prepared 3½" stems and four 2½" stems under the basted vine, overlapping the raw ends well so they'll be hidden; baste in place. Stitch the vines and stems. Working from the bottom layer to the top, continue positioning, basting, and stitching the remaining appliqués.

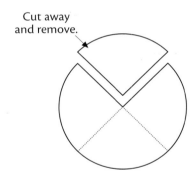

Cut away and remove.

5. For block 4, fold a prepared R flower appliqué in fourths as previously instructed and center it on the remaining block background. Referring to the quilt photo, tuck four prepared 7½" stems under the flower approximately ¼"; baste in place. Remove the flower appliqué. Stitch the stems in place. Reposition, baste, and stitch the flower. After removing the paper pattern piece, continue working from the bottom layer to the top to stitch the remaining appliqués.

6. For block 5, fold, crease and center the Y flower appliqué on the block background as previously instructed. Referring to the quilt photo, tuck two prepared 9" side stems under the flower

approximately ¼"; baste in place. Next, position two prepared 6" stems under the top and bottom edges of the Y flower; baste only the portion of the stems where they meet the flower in place, leaving the ends free to be pinned away from the seam area when the blocks are joined together. Stitch the Y appliqué in place, stitching over the stem ends to anchor them in place. Stitch the side stems only, and then remove the paper pattern piece from the flower. Working from the bottom layer to the top, continue positioning, basting, and stitching the remaining side appliqués and berries *only*. Reserve the remaining appliqués for the top and bottom stems for later use.

PIECING THE QUILT CENTER AND COMPLETING THE APPLIQUÉ

1. Referring to the illustration, lay out the blocks and two pieced sashing strips in three horizontal rows. Pin the unstitched stems in block 5 onto the flower appliqué so they won't be caught in the seams. Join the pieces in the top and bottom rows. Carefully press the seam allowances toward the sashing strips, taking care not to apply heat to the appliqués. Join the rows. Carefully press the seam allowances toward the block 5 center unit.

Block 1

Block 3

Block 5

Block 2

Block 4

2. Reposition, baste, and stitch the 6" stems onto the background of block 5. Work from the bottom layer to the top to position, baste, and stitch the reserved appliqués. The finished quilt center should now measure 51½" x 60½", including the seam allowances.

PIECING AND ADDING THE BORDERS

1. Join the assorted red print 2" strips to make a 240" length. From the pieced strip, cut 2 strips, 60½" long, and 2 strips, 54½" long. Sew a 60½" strip to the right and left sides of the quilt center. Carefully press the seam allowances toward the red strips. Join the 54½" strips to the top and bottom edges of the quilt center. Press the seam allowances toward the red strips.

2. Join 21 assorted medium to dark plaid 3½" x 6½" rectangles along the long edges to make a border strip. Press the seam allowances in one direction. Repeat for a total of two pieced strips. Join these strips to the right and left sides of the quilt top. Press the seam allowances toward the red inner border.

3. Join 18 assorted medium to dark plaid 3½" x 6½" rectangles along the long edges to make a border strip. Press the seam allowances in one direction. Repeat for a total of two pieced strips.

4. Join two assorted medium to dark plaid 6⅞" triangles along the long bias edges. Press the seam allowance to one side. Trim away the dog-ear points. Repeat for a total of four half-square-triangle units.

5. Join a half-square-triangle unit from step 4 to each end of the pieced border strips from step 3. Press the seam allowances toward the half-square-triangle units. Join these strips to the remaining edges of the quilt top. Press the seam allowances toward the red inner border. The quilt top should now measure 66½" x 75½", including the seam allowances.

COMPLETING THE QUILT

Refer to "Finishing Techniques" on page 19 for details as needed. Layer the quilt top, batting, and backing. Quilt the layers. The center of the featured quilt was machine quilted with an assortment of stylized shapes and swirls, and a running crescent motif was quilted around the red inner border. A meandering vine and leaf pattern was stitched onto the outer border. Join the assorted red print 2½"-wide random lengths into one length and use it to bind the quilt.

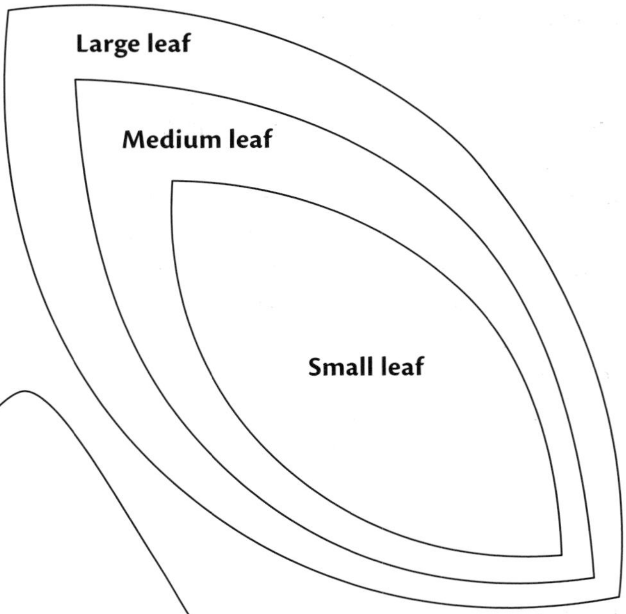

Large leaf

Medium leaf

Small leaf

B

Patterns do not include seam allowances.

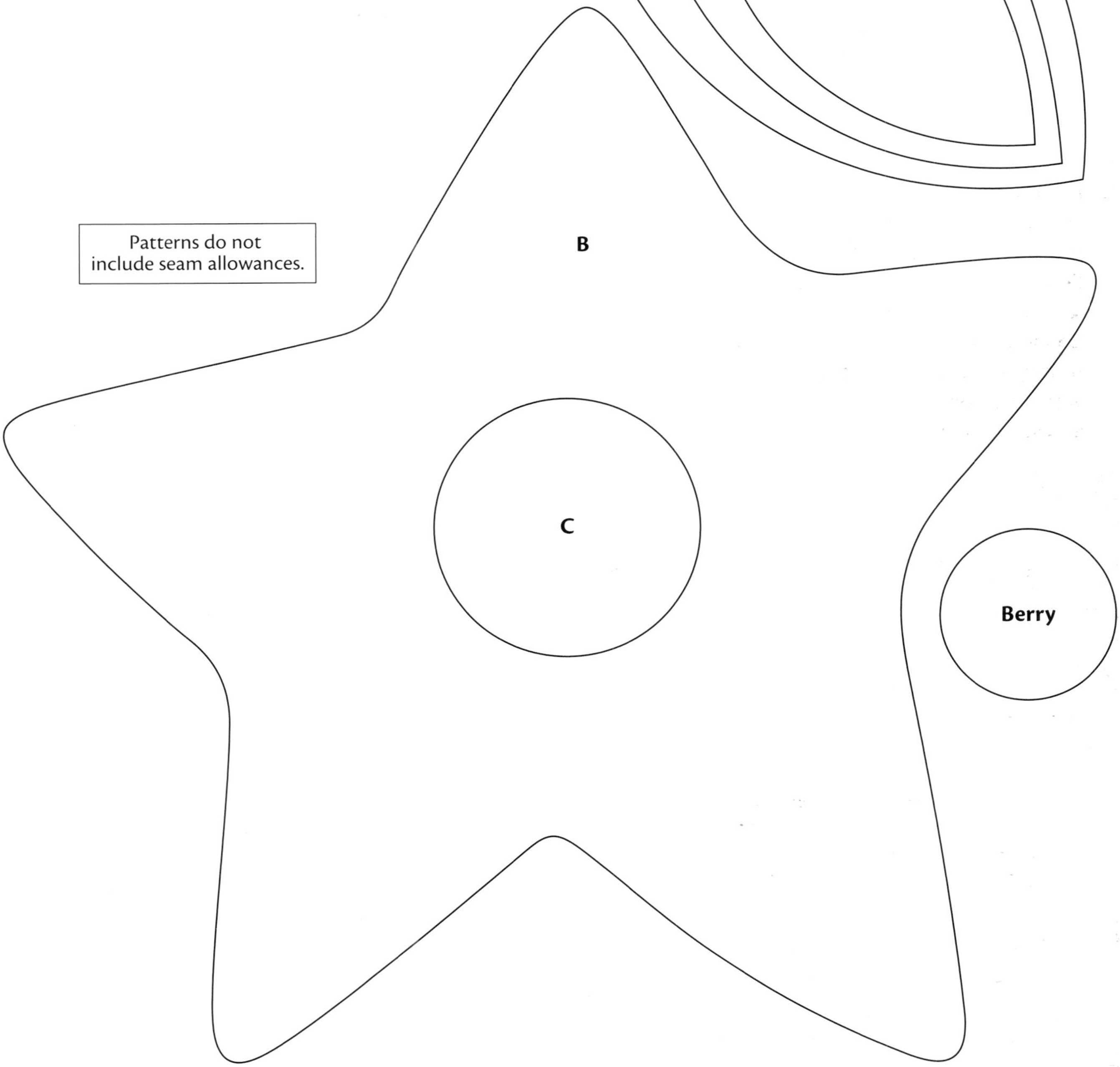

C

Berry

A
Cut pattern from
a 9" square of freezer paper
that has been folded in fourths.
Align dashed lines with folds.

Place on folds; do not cut through folds.

Place on folds; do not cut through folds.

F
*Note: The medium leaf
pattern can be substituted
for F to simplify the block.*

Patterns do not
include seam allowances.

D

E

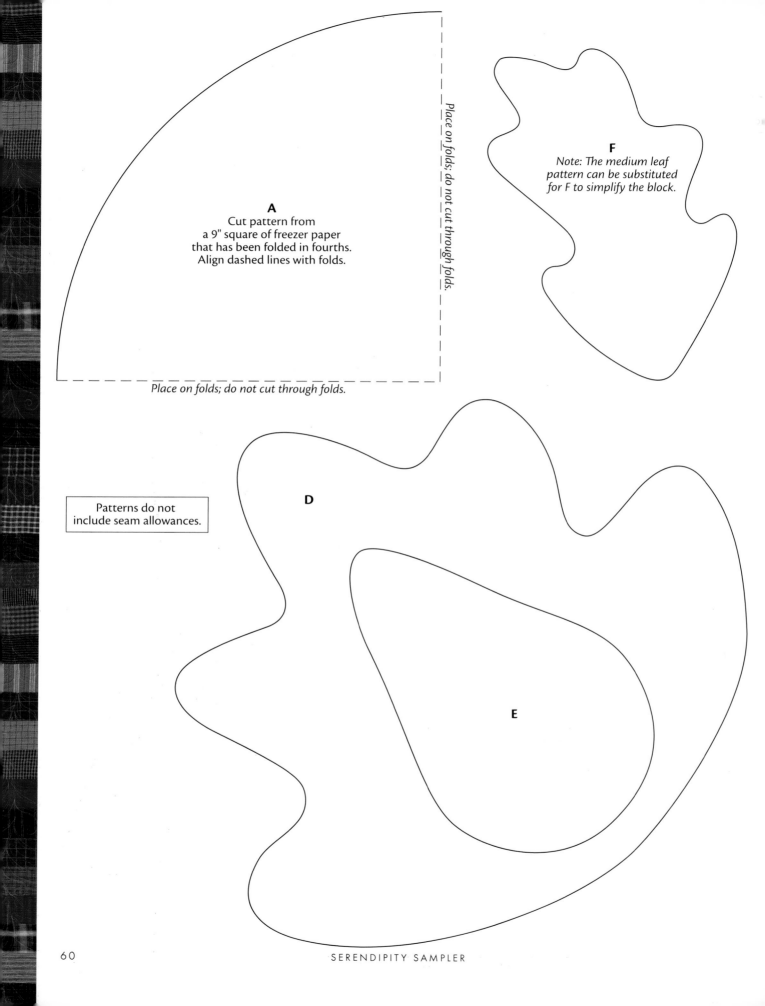

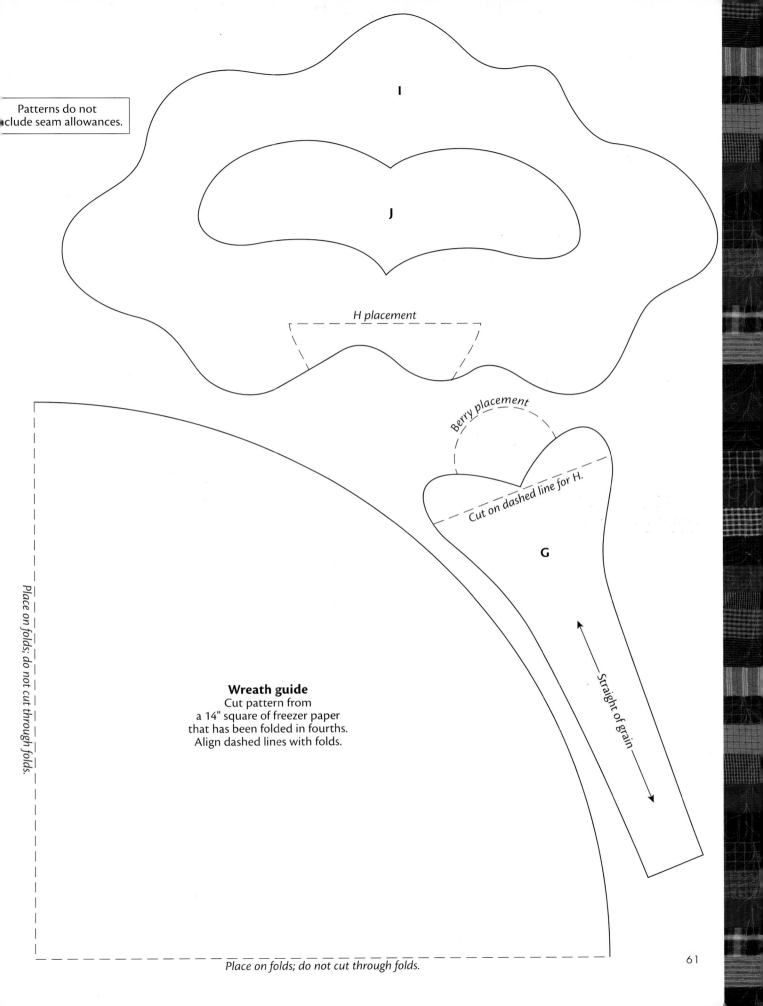

Patterns do not include seam allowances.

I

J

H placement

Berry placement

Cut on dashed line for H.

G

Straight of grain

Place on folds; do not cut through folds.

Wreath guide
Cut pattern from
a 14" square of freezer paper
that has been folded in fourths.
Align dashed lines with folds.

Place on folds; do not cut through folds.

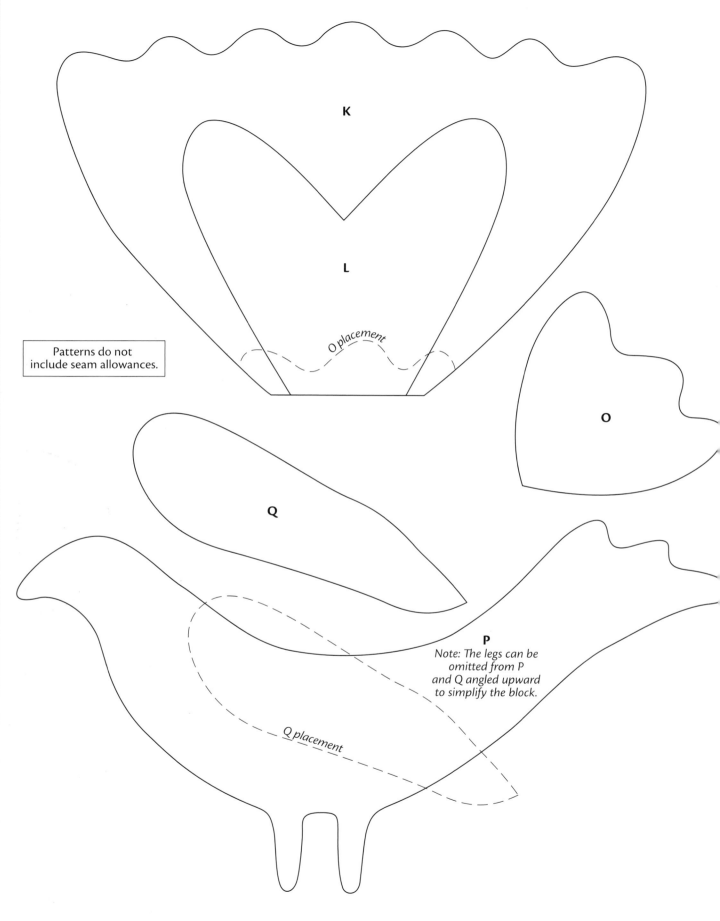

Patterns do not include seam allowances.

K

L

O placement

O

Q

Note: The legs can be omitted from P and Q angled upward to simplify the block.

P

Q placement

SERENDIPITY SAMPLER

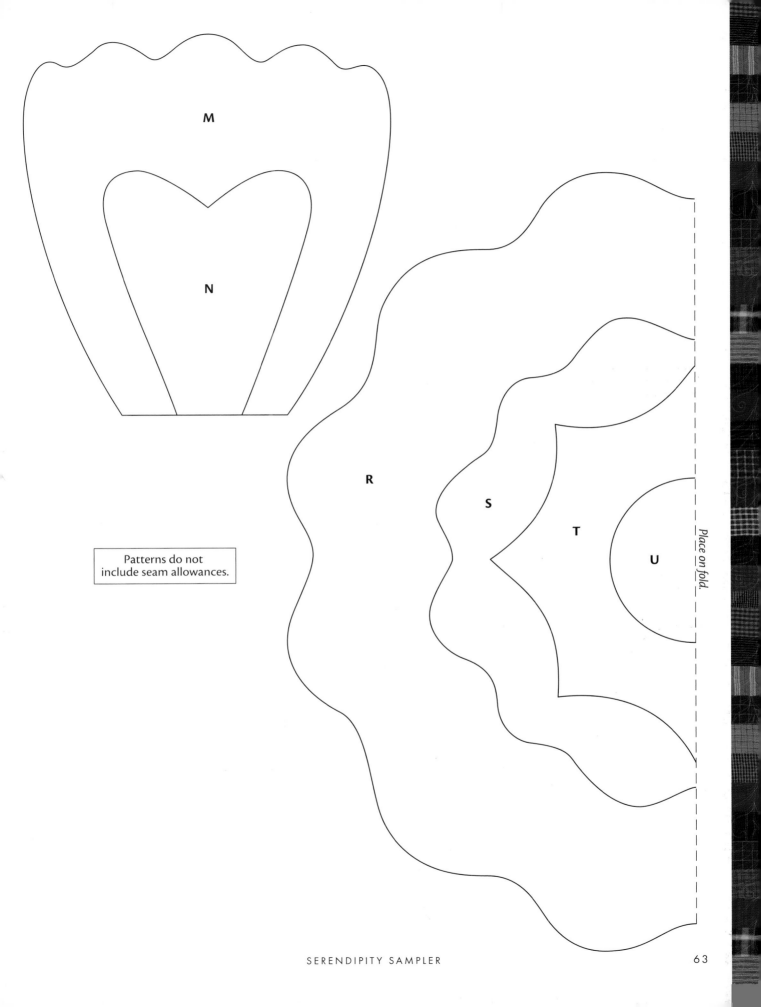

M

N

R

S

T

U

Patterns do not
include seam allowances.

Place on fold.

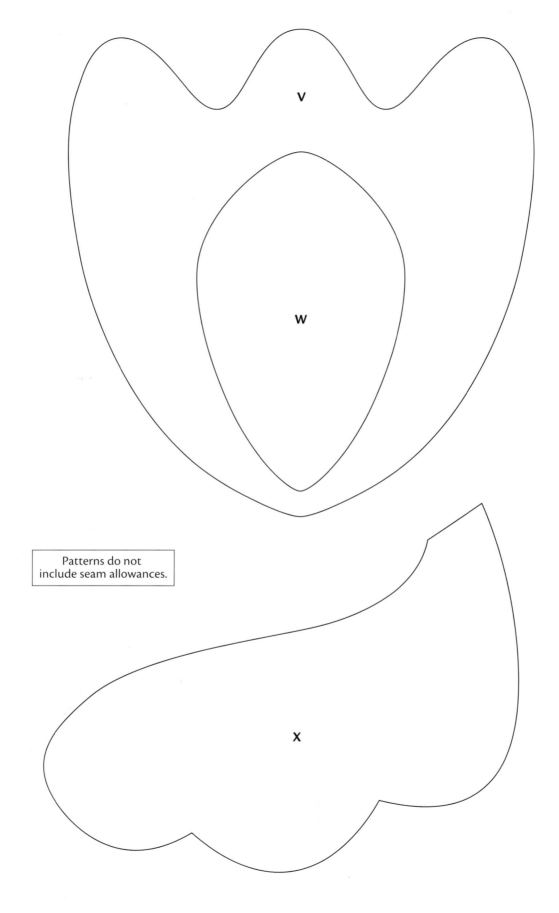

V

W

Patterns do not
include seam allowances.

X

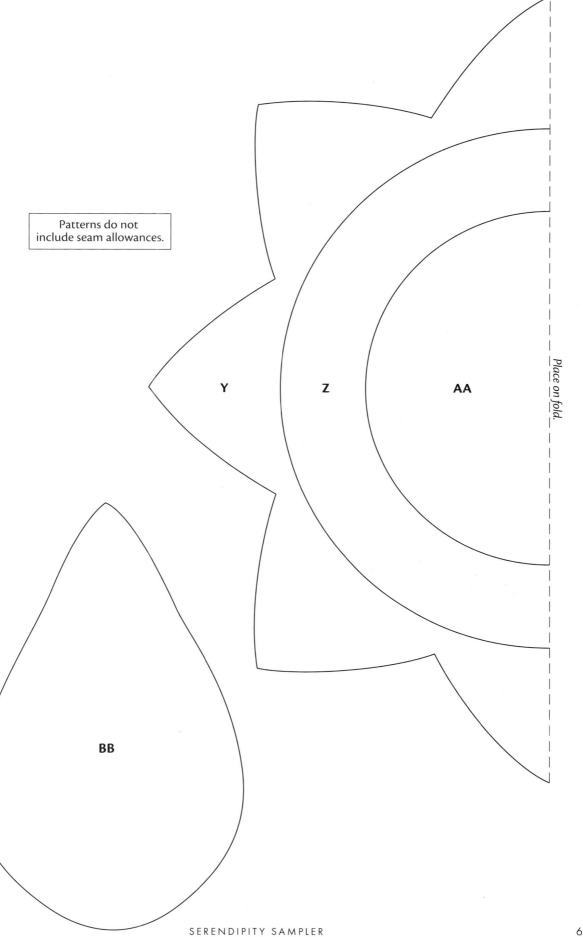

Patterns do not
include seam allowances.

Y

Z

AA

Place on fold.

BB

High Cotton

Harvest a bumper crop of your favorite prints while stitching this scrappy quilt chock-full of colorful checkerboard squares. Twisting and weaving ever upward to kiss the sky, these striking yet humble patchwork rows will brighten any room.

MATERIALS

32 fat eighths (9" x 22") of assorted medium and dark prints for blocks and border

4 fat quarters (18" x 22") of assorted neutral prints for blocks

4 squares (6½" x 6½") of assorted prints for border

⅝ yard of black print for binding

3½ yards of fabric for backing

61" x 73" piece of batting

CUTTING

Cut all pieces across the width of the fabric unless otherwise noted.

From the *longest edge* of *each* of the 32 assorted print fat eighths, cut:

1 strip, 1½" x 22" (combined total of 32)

1 strip, 6½" x 22"; crosscut into 1 square, 6½" x 6½" (combined total of 32). From the remainder of the strip, cut 2 lengthwise 2½"-wide strips; crosscut *each* of these strips into:

    2 rectangles, 2½" x 4½" (total of 4 from each print; combined total of 128)

    2 squares, 2½" x 2½" (total of 4 from each print; combined total of 128)

From the *longest edge* of *each* of the 4 assorted neutral print fat quarters, cut:

8 strips, 1½" x 22" (combined total of 32)

From the black print, cut:

7 strips, 2½" x 42" (binding)

PIECING THE BLOCKS

Sew all pieces with right sides together unless otherwise noted.

1. Select one assorted print 1½" x 22" strip and one neutral print 1½" x 22" strip. Stitch the pair together along one long edge to make a strip set. Press the seam allowances toward the assorted print. Repeat for a total of 32 strip sets. Crosscut *each* strip set into 12 segments, 1½" wide. Keep the segments from each strip set together.

1½"

Make 32 strip sets.
Cut 12 segments from each (384 total).

2. Join two matching segments as shown. Press the seam allowances to one side. Repeat for a total of six matching four-patch units from each assorted print measuring 2½" square, including the seam allowances.

Make 6
from each print.

3. Join a matching print 2½" x 4½" rectangle to a four-patch unit. Press the seam allowances toward the rectangle. Repeat for a total of four units from each print.

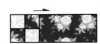

Make 4
from each print.

Finished quilt: 54½" x 66½" ■ Finished blocks: 6" x 6"
Designed by Kim Diehl. Pieced and machine quilted by Delene Kohler.

4. Join a matching print 2½" square to opposite sides of a four-patch unit. Press the seam allowances away from the four-patch unit. Repeat for a total of two units from each print.

Make 2
from each print.

5. Lay out two matching units from step 3 and one unit from step 4 to make a block. Join the rows. Press the seam allowances away from the middle row. Repeat for a total of 64 pieced blocks measuring 6½" square, including the seam allowances.

NOTE: The quilt center uses a total of 63 blocks, so there will be one extra block remaining when your quilt top is complete; having this extra block will give you added flexibility for color placement as the quilt center is pieced.

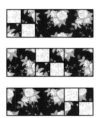 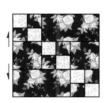

Make 64.

PIN POINT

Notched Spools

For thread spools that have a tiny notch for securing the end of your thread, try using a permanent marker to place a tiny dot at the notch; this will allow you to easily find it when your sewing is complete.

PIECING THE QUILT TOP

1. Lay out seven blocks and two assorted print 6½" squares as shown to form a row. Join the pieces.

Press the seam allowances in one direction. Repeat for a total of five A rows.

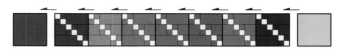

Row A.
Make 5.

2. Lay out seven blocks and two assorted print 6½" squares as shown to form a row. Be sure the blocks are rotated a quarter turn from the A row blocks. Press the seam allowances in the opposite direction as the A rows. Repeat for a total of four B rows.

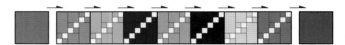

Row B.
Make 4.

3. Refer to the photo at left to lay out the rows. Join the rows. Press the seam allowances in one direction.

4. Join nine assorted print 6½" squares. Repeat for a total of two pieced border rows. Press the seam allowances of one row in the opposite direction of the pressed seam allowances in the first row of the quilt center. Press the seam allowances of the remaining border row in the opposite direction of the pressed seam allowances in the bottom row of the quilt center. Join these pieced border rows to the top and bottom edge of the quilt center. Press the seam allowances toward the border rows. The pieced quilt top should now measure 54½" x 66½", including the seam allowances.

COMPLETING THE QUILT

Refer to "Finishing Techniques" on page 19 for details as needed. Layer the quilt top, batting, and backing. Quilt the layers. The featured quilt was machine quilted in an overall swirling pattern as provided in "Machine Quilting" on page 20. Join the seven black print 2½" x 42½" strips into one length and use it to bind the quilt.

Peas in a Pod

Snap some fresh peas straight from your stash with this winsome
quilt in an abundance of sun-warmed colors. So good for you
and delicious, you'll be sure to ask for seconds!

MATERIALS

60 chubby sixteenths (9" x 11") *or* 4 yards
  total of assorted prints for blocks, border,
  and binding

2 yards of light blue print for blocks

3¼ yards of fabric for backing

56" x 66" piece of batting

CUTTING

Cut all pieces across the width of the fabric
unless otherwise noted. Refer to page 75 for
appliqué pattern A and to "Invisible Machine
Appliqué" beginning on page 10 for pattern
piece preparation.

From the light blue print, cut:

12 strips, 1½" x 42"; crosscut into:

  50 rectangles, 1½" x 8"

  50 squares, 1½" x 1½"

8 strips, 5½" x 42"; crosscut into 49 squares,
  5½" x 5½"

**From *each* of 25 of the assorted print chubby
sixteenths, cut:**

8 squares, 2½" x 2½" (combined total of
  200). Reserve the scraps for appliqués and
  borders.

*For greater ease in piecing, keep the squares
organized by print.*

**From the *longest edge* of *each* of 25 different
assorted print chubby sixteenths, cut:**

2 rectangles, 1½" x 8" (combined total of
  50). Reserve the scraps for appliqués and
  borders.

PIN POINT

Successful Scrap Quilts

When choosing fabrics for scrappy
quilts, make sure they are all of a similar weight and weave. This will ensure
that the finished quilt is uniform in
texture and that your pressed seams
will lie flat and smooth.

**From the remaining chubby sixteenths *and*
the reserved chubby sixteenth scraps, cut:**

178 using pattern A. (Please note that it isn't
  necessary to add a seam allowance to the
  straight edge of each appliqué; this edge
  will be enclosed within the block seam.)

Enough 1½"-wide random lengths to make 2
  strips, 55½" each (border 1)

Enough 1½"-wide random lengths to make
  2 strips, 47½" each (border 1)

Enough 1½"-wide random lengths to make 2
  strips, 57½" each (border 2)

Enough 1½"-wide random lengths to make
  2 strips, 49½" each (border 2)

Enough 2½"-wide random lengths to make a
  228" length of binding when joined end
  to end

Finished quilt: 49½" x 59½" ■ Finished blocks: 5" x 5"

Designed and machine appliquéd by Kim Diehl.
Pieced by Deb Behrend and Kim Diehl. Machine quilted by Celeste Freiberg.

PIECING THE NINE PATCH VARIATION BLOCKS

Sew all pieces with right sides together unless otherwise noted.

1. Select a light blue print and assorted print 1½" x 8" rectangle. Stitch the pair together along one long edge to make a strip set. Press the seam allowance toward the assorted print. Repeat for a total of 50 strip sets. Crosscut *each* strip set into four segments, 1½" wide. Keep the segments from each strip set together.

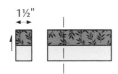

2. Lay out one matching set of four strip-set segments, four matching 2½" squares cut from a different assorted print than the strip-set segments, and one light blue print 1½" square to form a block. Join the pieces in each horizontal row. Press the seam allowances of the top and bottom rows toward the assorted print 2½" squares. Press the seam allowances of the middle row toward the light blue center square. Join the rows. Press the seam allowances away from the center row. Repeat for a total of 50 Nine Patch Variation blocks measuring 5½" square, including the seam allowances.

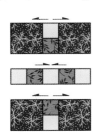 

Make 50.

STITCHING THE APPLIQUÉ BLOCKS

1. Fold a light blue print 5½" square in half right sides together and lightly press a horizontal center crease. Refold vertically and lightly press a second crease. Repeat for a total of 49 pressed background squares.

Creased block.
Make 49.

2. Fold each prepared A appliqué in half crosswise and gently finger-press a center crease.

3. Randomly select four prepared A appliqués. Position one appliqué on each side of a prepared 5½" background square, lining up the pressed creases to center each one and aligning the raw edges. Baste the appliqués in place. Referring to "Stitching the Appliqués" on page 15, stitch the appliqués to the background. Remove the paper pattern pieces as instructed in "Removing Paper Pattern Pieces" on page 16. Repeat for a total of 31 appliquéd A blocks.

Block A.
Make 31.

4. Referring to step 3, make a total of 18 appliquéd B blocks containing one unappliquéd side per block.

Block B.
Make 18.

PIECING THE QUILT CENTER

1. Lay out five Nine Patch Variation blocks and four appliquéd B blocks as shown. Join the blocks. Carefully press the seam allowances toward the Nine Patch Variation blocks, taking care not to apply heat to the appliqués. Repeat for a total of two A rows.

Row A.
Make 2.

2. Lay out four Nine Patch Variation blocks, three appliquéd A blocks, and two appliquéd B blocks as shown. Join the blocks. Carefully press the seam allowances toward the Nine Patch Variation blocks. Repeat for a total of five B rows.

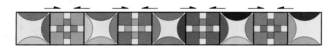

Row B.
Make 5.

PIN POINT

Cutting Multiple Paper Pattern Pieces without Pinning

To eliminate pinning freezer-paper layers after the appliqué shape has been traced, try holding the tip of a hot iron to the topmost paper layer at spaced intervals around the shape, at least ¼" *outside* the drawn lines. Hold the iron in place until the layers are fused, and then cut out the shape.

3. Lay out five Nine Patch Variation blocks and four appliquéd A blocks as shown. Join the blocks. Carefully press the seam allowances toward the Nine Patch Variation blocks. Repeat for a total of four C rows.

Row C.
Make 4.

4. Lay out the rows as shown. Join the rows. Carefully press the seam allowances toward the A and C rows. The pieced quilt center should now measure 45½" x 55½", including the seam allowances.

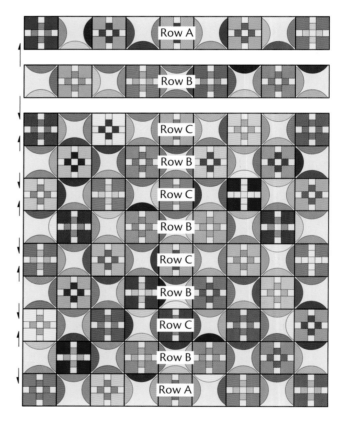

PIECING AND ADDING THE BORDERS

1. Join the random lengths of assorted print 1½"-wide strips using straight seams to make two *each* of the border strip lengths designated in "Cutting" on page 71. Press the seam allowances in one direction.

2. Join a pieced 55½" border strip to the right and left sides of the quilt center. Press the seam allowances toward the border strips. Join a pieced 47½" border strip to the top and bottom edges of the quilt center. Press the seam allowances toward the border strips.

3. Join a pieced 57½" border strip to the right and left sides of the quilt top. Press the seam allowances toward the border strips. Join a 49½" pieced border strip to the remaining sides of the quilt top. Press the seam allowances toward the border strips. The pieced quilt top should now measure 49½" x 59½", including the seam allowances.

COMPLETING THE QUILT

Refer to "Finishing Techniques" on page 19 for details as needed. Layer the quilt top, batting, and backing. Quilt the layers. The featured quilt was machine quilted with an X stitched onto the light blue center square of each Nine Patch Variation block; feathered wreaths were quilted around the block centers, extending onto the curved appliqué crescents. The background areas of the appliqué blocks were quilted with four intersecting teardrop shapes and the open areas were filled in with a tiny stipple design. The borders were quilted with a gently curved repeating S shape to form a running cable. Join the random lengths of assorted print 2½"-wide strips into one length and use it to bind the quilt.

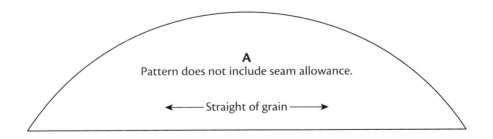

A
Pattern does not include seam allowance.

← Straight of grain →

Thistle Thicket

Plant your very own secret garden with a scattering of tassle-topped thistles and dew-drenched berries, and then border your appliquéd haven with checkerboard cobblestones in a rainbow of colors.

MATERIALS

2⅛ yards of cream print for center block checkerboard center, and checkerboard border

16 fat eighths (9" x 22") of assorted prints for checkerboard center and border

2 yards of red print for appliqués and outer border

1 yard of light green print for appliqués and binding

1 fat quarter (18" x 22") of medium green print for appliqués

1 fat quarter (18" x 22") of cranberry print for appliqués

1 fat eighth (9" x 22") of medium lavender print for appliqués

1 square, 6" x 6", of coordinating lavender print for appliqués

4 yards of fabric for backing

67" x 67" square of batting

Fine-point water-soluble marker

CUTTING

Cut all pieces across the width of the fabric unless otherwise noted. Refer to pages 83–85 for appliqué patterns A–K and to "Invisible Machine Appliqué" beginning on page 10 for pattern piece preparation.

From the cream print, cut:
1 square, 40½" x 40½"

16 strips, 1½" x 42"; cut each strip in half crosswise to make a total of 32 strips, 1½" x 21"

From *each* of the 16 fat eighths of assorted prints, cut:
2 strips, 1½" x 21" (combined total of 32)

From the *lengthwise grain* of the red print, cut:
2 strips, 6½" x 48½"
2 strips, 6½" x 60½"

From the remaining red print, cut:
1 using pattern A
20 using pattern K
20 using pattern J
20 using pattern J reversed
16 using pattern H
4 using pattern I

PIN POINT

Buttons for Berries

To simplify appliqué projects featuring berries, consider substituting a variety of buttons. They can be sewn to your quilt top using decorative threads and stitches, and they produce quick and perfect results. I find that this option is best for wall hangings or quilts that won't be used by small children.

Finished quilt: 60½" x 60½" ■ Finished center: 40" x 40"
Designed, pieced, and machine appliquéd by Kim Diehl. Machine quilted by Celeste Freiberg.

From the light green print, cut:

2 strips, 1½" x 42"; crosscut into:

    4 strips, 1½" x 7"

    4 strips, 1½" x 5"

1 strip, 3½" x 42"; crosscut into 2 rectangles, 3½" x 14"

7 strips, 2½" x 42" (binding)

4 using pattern D

4 using pattern D reversed

6 using pattern F

6 using pattern F reversed

From the medium green print, cut:

4 using pattern E

4 using pattern E reversed

2 using pattern F

2 using pattern F reversed

From the cranberry print, cut:

4 using pattern C

4 using pattern I

4 using pattern J

4 using pattern J reversed

From the *longest edge* of the medium lavender print fat eighth, cut:

2 rectangles, 3½" x 14"

From the remaining lavender print fat eighth and the 6" square of coordinating lavender print, cut a *combined total* of:

24 using pattern H

PIECING THE CHECKERBOARD UNITS

Sew all pieces with right sides together unless otherwise noted.

1. Select an assorted print 1½" x 21" strip and a cream print 1½" x 21" strip. Stitch the pair together along one long edge. Press the seam allowances toward the assorted print. Repeat for a total of 32 pieced strips.

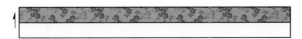

Make 32.

2. Select two pieced strips. Join the pair as shown. Press the seam allowances toward the assorted print. Repeat for a total of 16 strip sets. Crosscut the strip sets into 192 segments, 1½" wide.

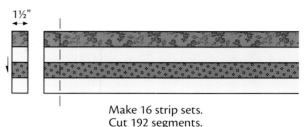

Make 16 strip sets.
Cut 192 segments.

3. Join eight strip-set segments as shown to make a checkerboard rectangle unit. Press the seam allowances in one direction. Repeat to make a second checkerboard rectangle unit; press the seam allowances in the opposite direction. Join the units to make a checkerboard square. Press the seam allowance open.

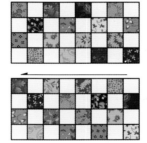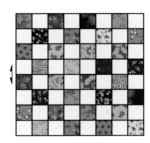

4. Join 40 strip-set segments from step 2 as shown, noting the position of the cream and assorted print squares in the first segment, to make a checkerboard strip. Press the seam allowances in one direction. Repeat for a total of two short checkerboard strips.

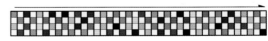

Make 2.

5. Repeat step 4 using 48 strip-set segments from step 2, and again noting the placement of the first segment to position the cream and assorted print squares correctly. Repeat for a total of two long checkerboard strips.

Make 2.

6. Reserve the short and long checkerboard strips from steps 4 and 5 for use in the middle border.

PREPARING THE CHECKERBOARD AND THISTLE APPLIQUÉS

1. Fold the checkerboard square from step 3 of "Piecing the Checkerboard Units" vertically, offsetting the fold so that it runs through the squares just to one side of the center seam; press. In the same manner, refold and press a horizontal crease. With the waxy side up, align the creases of the B pattern piece with the creases on the *wrong* side of the checkerboard square and use a small amount of fabric glue stick to anchor it in place. Cut out the appliqué, adding a generous ¼" seam allowance. Press the seam allowance onto the waxy side of the pattern piece.

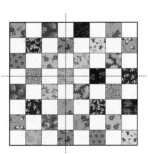

Crease the checkerboard.

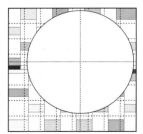

2. To prepare the G appliqués, join a light green and medium lavender print 3½" x 14" rectangle along the long edges. Press the seam allowances toward the green print. Repeat for a total of two pieced rectangles. Position two G pattern pieces onto the wrong side of a pieced rectangle, waxy side up, aligning the dashed lines of the pattern with the seam line of the rectangle; anchor it in place with a small amount of fabric glue stick. Cut out the appliqués, adding a scant ¼" seam allowance, and press as previously instructed. Repeat for a total of four prepared G appliqués.

APPLIQUÉING THE QUILT CENTER

1. With right sides together, fold the cream print square in half and lightly press a center vertical crease. Refold and press the square to add horizontal and diagonal creases. Next, measure in 5¼" from one raw edge and use a clear acrylic ruler and water-soluble marker to draw a line, starting and stopping about 3" from each end. Repeat with the remaining sides of the square (the lines at each corner should intersect).

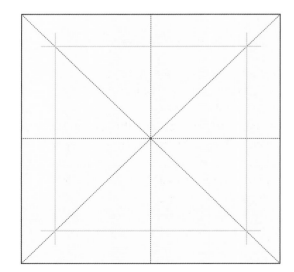

2. Referring to "Making Bias-Tube Stems and Vines" on page 13, prepare the light green 1½" x 7" and 1½" x 5" strips.

3. Carefully fold the prepared A appliqué in half vertically and horizontally and finger-press the creases. Line up these creases with the creases on the block background; pin or baste the appliqué in place. Dot the seam allowances of the prepared 7" stems with liquid basting glue at 1" intervals. Press the stems onto the background, centering them over the diagonal creases and tucking the raw ends under the A appliqué approximately ¼". In the same manner, glue baste and position the prepared 5" stems onto the background, centering them over the vertical and horizontal creases. Referring to "Stitching the Appliqués" on page 15, stitch the A appliqué to the background. Referring to "Removing Paper Pattern Pieces" on page 16, remove the paper pattern piece.

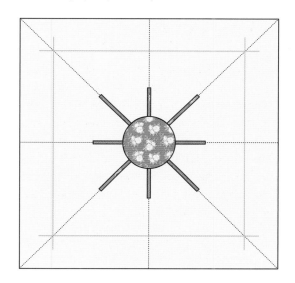

4. Referring to the quilt photo, position and baste a prepared C appliqué onto each diagonal stem and a prepared G appliqué onto each vertical and horizontal stem, overlapping the raw ends by approximately ¼". Center and baste the prepared B appliqué onto the A appliqué. Stitch the appliqués in place and remove the paper pattern pieces. Do not stitch the stems at this time.

5. Position and baste a D and E appliqué onto the right-hand side of each diagonal stem and a D and E reversed appliqué onto the left-hand sides, tucking the raw ends under the stems. Stitch the appliqués and all stems in place. Remove the paper pattern pieces.

6. Position, baste, and stitch the F and F reversed appliqués and the lavender print H appliqués along the stems. Remove the paper pattern pieces.

7. Position, baste, and stitch a cranberry print I, J, and J reversed appliqué just beyond the appliqués at the end of each diagonal stem. Remove the paper pattern pieces.

8. Beginning at the position where the water-soluble lines intersect at one corner of the background square, position a prepared K appliqué with the pointed ends resting on the drawn line. In the same manner, position a second prepared K appliqué at the opposite end of the drawn line. Working from each end to the middle, add three more K appliqués, positioning them to fill the space evenly and overlapping as necessary to fit them to your liking; baste in place. Position and baste a prepared J, J reversed, and H appliqué at the juncture where each K appliqué meets. Repeat with the remaining sides of the quilt center. Stitch the appliqués in place. Remove the paper pattern pieces.

Appliqué placement diagram

9. Position, baste, and stitch an I, J, and J reversed appliqué to each appliquéd corner of the quilt center. Remove the paper pattern pieces.

10. Use a damp piece of muslin or white paper towel to remove the marked water-soluble lines.

ADDING THE BORDERS

1. Referring to the quilt photo for placement, join short checkerboard strips to the right and left sides of the quilt center. Press the seam allowances toward the checkerboard strips. In the same manner, join and press a long checkerboard strip to each remaining side of the quilt center.

2. Join red print 6½" x 48½" strips to the right and left sides of the quilt top. Press the seam allowances toward the red print. Join a red print 6½" x 60½" strip to each remaining side of the quilt top. Press the seam allowances toward the red print. The pieced quilt top should measure 60½" square, including the seam allowances.

COMPLETING THE QUILT

Refer to "Finishing Techniques" on page 19 for details as needed. Layer the quilt top, batting, and backing. Quilt the layers. The featured quilt was machine quilted with a feathered wreath on the red circular A appliqué. Xs were stitched onto all checkerboard patchwork and the open background areas were quilted with a stipple design. The red outer border was stitched with a meandering feathered cable. Join the seven green print 2½" x 42" strips into one length and use it to bind the quilt.

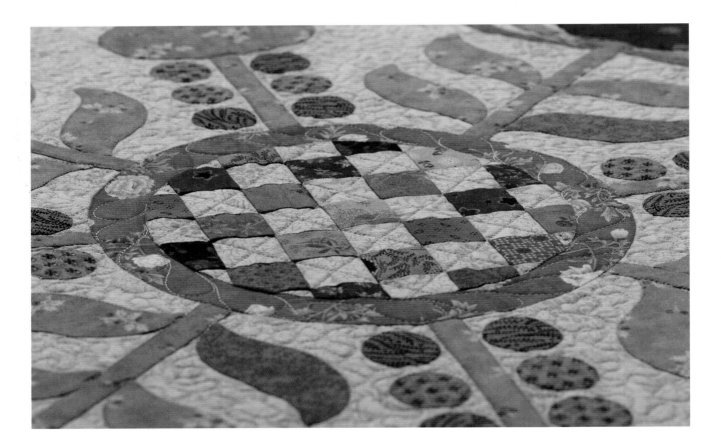

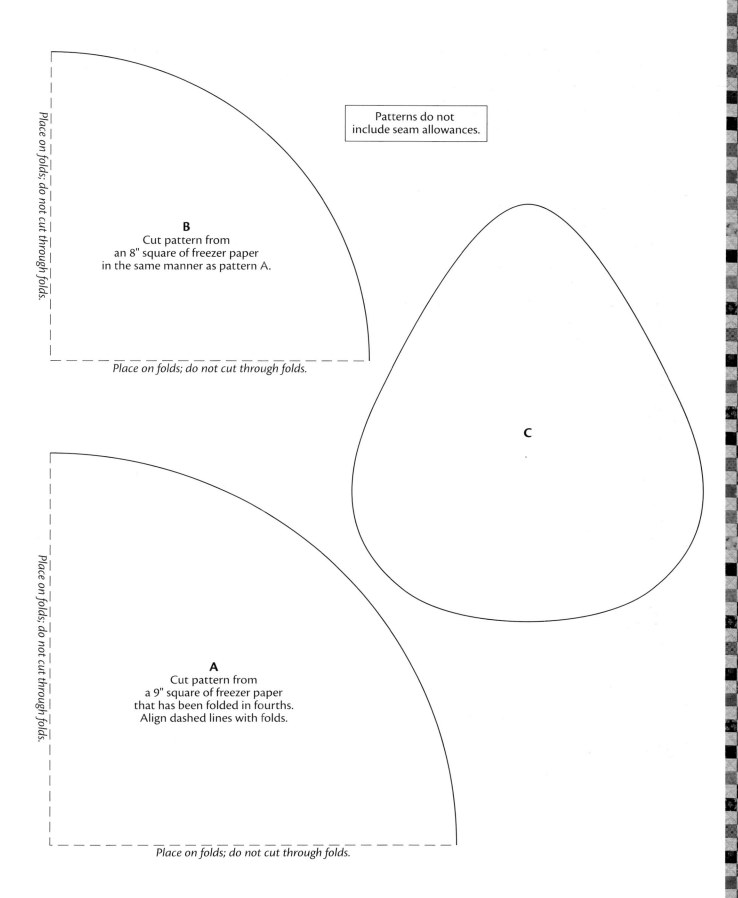

Place on folds; do not cut through folds.

Patterns do not include seam allowances.

B
Cut pattern from
an 8" square of freezer paper
in the same manner as pattern A.

Place on folds; do not cut through folds.

C

A
Cut pattern from
a 9" square of freezer paper
that has been folded in fourths.
Align dashed lines with folds.

Place on folds; do not cut through folds.

Place on folds; do not cut through folds.

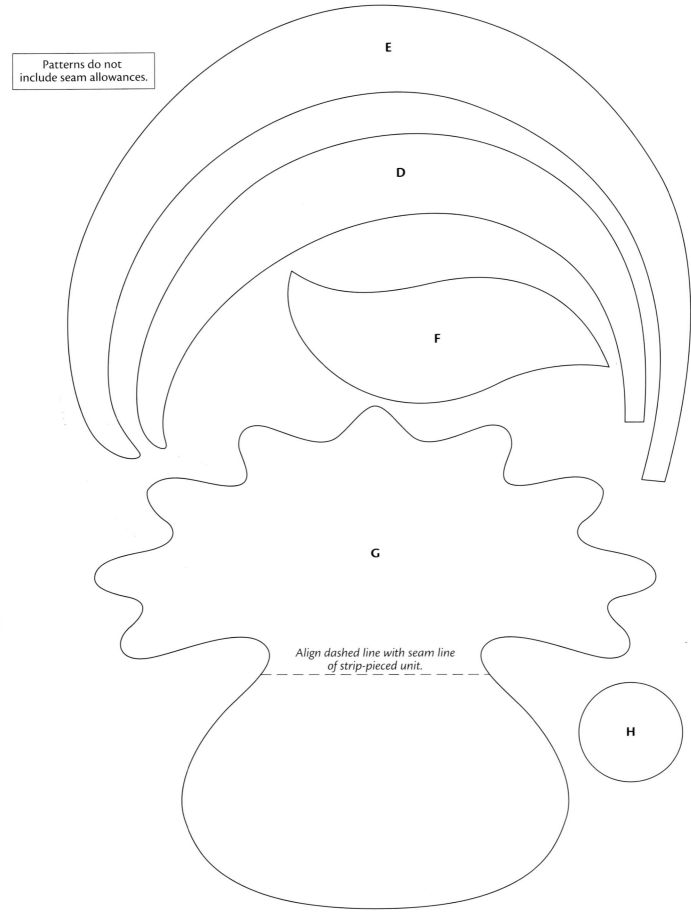

Patterns do not include seam allowances.

E

D

F

G

Align dashed line with seam line of strip-pieced unit.

H

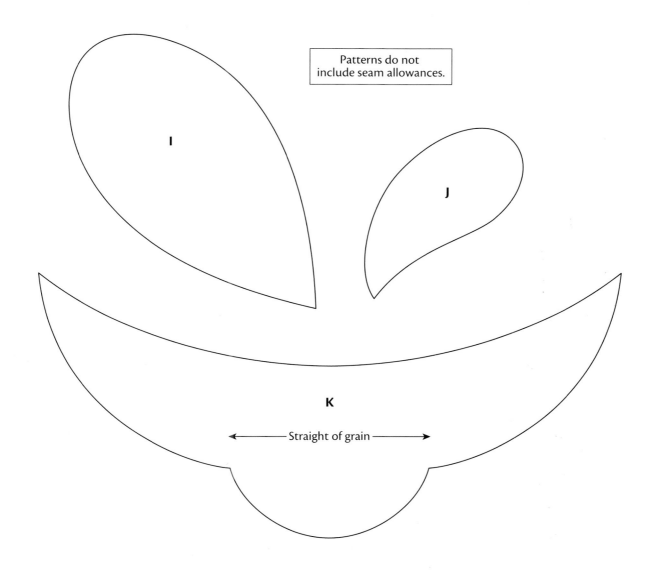

Patterns do not include seam allowances.

I

J

K

← Straight of grain →

Twilight Hopscotch

Twinkling stars appear to be just a hop, a skip, and a jump away as
they dance through the milky twilight in this traditionally designed quilt.
Quiet yet eloquent, these simply pieced stars will shine in any setting.

MATERIALS

3½ yards of cream print for block background
and sashing

1½ yards of medium green print for blocks
(stars) and binding

1⅛ yards of coordinating medium green print
for blocks (small diagonal corner squares)
and sashing squares

4 yards of fabric for backing

69" x 69" square of batting

CUTTING

Cut all pieces across the width of the fabric
unless otherwise noted.

From the medium green print for stars, cut:
8 strips, 2½" x 42"; crosscut into 128 squares,
   2½" x 2½"

2 strips, 4½" x 42"; crosscut into 16 squares,
   4½" x 4½"

7 strips, 2½" x 42" (binding)

From the cream print, cut:
8 strips, 4½" x 42"; crosscut into 64 squares,
   4½" x 4½"

10 strips, 1½" x 42"

26 strips, 2½" x 42"; crosscut into:
   157 squares, 2½" x 2½"
   40 rectangles, 2½" x 8½"
   16 rectangles, 2½" x 12½"

**From the coordinating green print for corner
squares, cut:**
10 strips, 1½" x 42"

7 strips, 2½" x 42"; crosscut into 100 squares,
   2½" x 2½"

Finished quilt: 62½" x 62½" ■ Finished blocks: 12" x 12"
Designed by Kim Diehl. Pieced by Deb Behrend. Machine quilted by Delene Kohler.

PIECING THE STAR BLOCKS

Sew all pieces with right sides together unless otherwise noted.

1. Lightly draw a diagonal line on the wrong side of each of the 128 green print 2½" squares designated for the stars.

2. Layer a prepared square onto one corner of a cream print 4½" square; stitch the pair together exactly on the drawn line. Referring to "Pressing Triangle Units" on page 10, press and trim the star point. In the same manner, sew, press, and trim a second prepared green print 2½" square, placing it in a mirror-image position. Repeat for a total of 64 star point units.

Make 64.

3. Sew each cream print 1½" x 42" strip to a coordinating green print 1½" x 42" strip along one long edge to make a strip set. Press the seam allowances toward the green print. Repeat for a total of 10 strip sets. Crosscut the strip sets into 256 segments, 1½" wide.

1½"

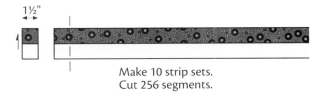

Make 10 strip sets.
Cut 256 segments.

4. Join two strip-set segments as shown to make a four-patch unit. Press the seam allowances to one side. Repeat for a total of 128 four-patch units measuring 2½" square.

Make 128.

5. Lay out two four-patch units and two cream print 2½" squares as shown. Join the pieces in each horizontal row. Press the seam allowances toward the cream print. Join the rows. Press the seam allowances to one side. Repeat for a total of 64 corner units.

Make 64.

6. Lay out four star point units from step 2, four corner units from step 5, and one green print 4½" square as shown. Join the pieces in each horizontal row. Press the seam allowances away from the star point units. Join the rows. Press the seam allowances away from the middle row. Repeat for a total of 16 Star blocks measuring 12½" square, including the seam allowances.

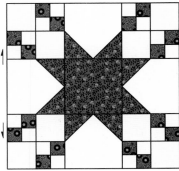

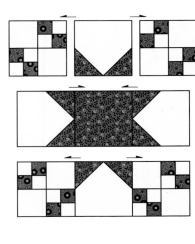

Make 16.

PIECING THE QUILT-CENTER SASHING UNITS

Join a coordinating green print 2½" square to each end of a cream print 2½" x 8½" rectangle. Press the seam allowances toward the cream print. Repeat for a total of 40 pieced sashing units.

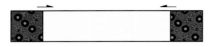

Make 40.

PIECING THE QUILT CENTER

1. Lay out four Star blocks and five sashing units in alternating positions. Join the pieces. Press the seam allowances toward the sashing units. Repeat for a total of four block rows.

Make 4.

2. Lay out four sashing units and five cream print 2½" squares in alternating positions. Join the pieces. Press the seam allowances away from the cream print squares. Repeat for a total of five sashing rows.

Make 5.

3. Lay out five sashing rows and four block rows in alternating positions. Join the rows. Press the seam allowances toward the sashing rows. The pieced quilt center should now measure 58½" square, including the seam allowances.

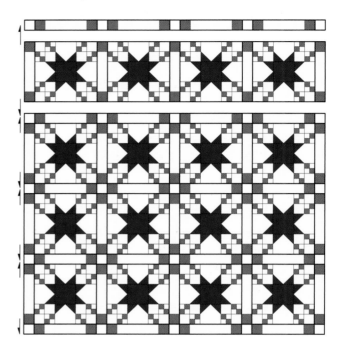

PIECING AND ADDING THE OUTER SASHING BORDER

1. Lay out five coordinating green print 2½" squares and four cream print 2½" x 12½" rectangles in alternating positions. Join the pieces. Press the seam allowances toward the green print. Repeat for a total of four pieced sashing strips.

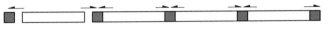

Make 4.

2. Join a pieced sashing strip to the right and left sides of the quilt center, reserving two strips for step 3. Press the seam allowances away from the quilt center.

3. Join a cream print 2½" square to each end of the reserved sashing strips. Press the seam allowances toward the green print. Sew these strips to the remaining edges of the quilt center. Press the seam allowances away from the quilt center. The pieced quilt top should now measure 62½" square, including the seam allowances.

COMPLETING THE QUILT

Refer to "Finishing Techniques" on page 19 for details as needed. Layer the quilt top, batting, and backing. Quilt the layers. The featured quilt was machine quilted in the ditch along the Star block seams, with on-point squares and swags placed in the center of each star. Xs were quilted onto each green print setting square and feathered Xs were stitched on point in the background areas. A tiny stipple design was used to fill the open background areas around the feathered motifs. Join the seven green print 2½" x 42" strips into one length and use it to bind the quilt.

Checkerberry Bliss

All roads lead to bliss as you fashion rows of gently furrowed Four Patch blocks, and then surround them with baskets of blossoms and berries ripe for the picking. Set against a backdrop of soft midnight sky, these garden glories will forever be in bloom.

MATERIALS

2⅞ yards of black print (with a subtle design) for blocks, border, and binding

1⅝ yards of medium green print for blocks, border, and appliqués

⅞ yard of cream print for blocks and appliqués

½ yard of muted gold print for appliqués

½ yard of medium-dark green print for vines and appliqués

1 fat eighth (9" x 22") *each* of medium brown and coordinating medium green print for appliqués

7 chubby sixteenths (9" x 11") *total* of assorted muted red, pink, lavender, blue, and orange prints for appliqués

4 yards of fabric for backing

67" x 67" square of batting

⅜" bias bar

CUTTING

Cut all pieces across the width of the fabric unless otherwise noted. Refer to page 97 for appliqué patterns A–F and to "Invisible Machine Appliqué" beginning on page 10 for pattern piece preparation.

From the medium green print, cut:

9 strips, 3½" x 42"; crosscut into 98 squares, 3½" x 3½"

1 strip, 9½" x 42"; crosscut into 4 squares, 9½" x 9½"

Reserve the remaining scraps for the leaf appliqués.

From the *bias* of the medium-dark green print, cut:

12 rectangles, 1¼" x 2½"

16 rectangles, 1¼" x 4½"

8 strips, 1¼" x 18"

8 strips, 1¼" x 15"

From the remaining medium-dark green print, the fat eighth of coordinating green print, and scraps of medium green print, cut a *combined total* of:

64 using a random mix of patterns E and E reversed

From the cream print, cut:

10 strips, 2" x 42"

88 using pattern F

From the *lengthwise grain* of the black print, cut:

4 strips, 9½" x 42½"

From the remaining black print, cut:

10 strips, 2" x 42"

7 strips, 2½" x 42" (binding)

12 using pattern B

From the medium brown print, cut:

4 using pattern A

From the muted gold print, cut:

28 using pattern C

From *each* of the 7 assorted muted red, pink, lavender, blue, and orange prints, cut:

4 using pattern D (combined total of 28)

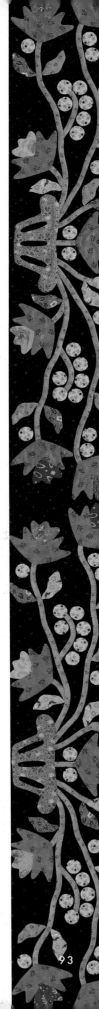

Finished quilt: 60½" x 60½" ■ Finished blocks: 6" x 6"
Designed and machine appliquéd by Kim Diehl. Pieced by Deslynn Mecham and Kim Diehl.
Machine quilted by Celeste Freiberg.

CHECKERBERRY BLISS

PIECING THE FOUR PATCH VARIATION BLOCKS

Sew all pieces with right sides together unless otherwise noted.

1. Sew each cream print 2" x 42" strip to a black print 2" x 42" strip along one long edge to make a strip set. Press the seam allowances toward the black print. Repeat for a total of 10 strip sets. Crosscut the strip sets into 196 segments, 2" wide.

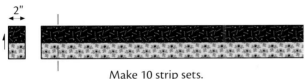

Make 10 strip sets.
Cut 196 segments.

2. Join two strip-set segments as shown to make a four-patch unit. Press the seam allowance to one side. Repeat for a total of 98 four-patch units measuring 3½" square, including the seam allowances.

    NOTE: Take care that all of the four-patch units are assembled with the pieces consistently positioned as shown; this will help ensure that your finished quilt center duplicates the pattern of the featured quilt.

Make 98.

3. Lay out two four-patch units and two green print 3½" squares. Join the pieces in each horizontal row. Press the seam allowances toward the green print. Join the rows. Press the seam allowances to one side. Repeat for a total of 49 Four Patch Variation blocks measuring 6½" square, including the seam allowances.

Make 49.

ASSEMBLING THE QUILT CENTER

1. Lay out seven Four Patch Variation blocks, turning every other block to position the center seams in opposing directions. Join the blocks. Press the seam allowances in one direction. Repeat for a total of seven pieced rows.

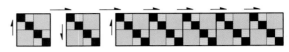

Make 7.

2. Lay out the pieced rows, turning every other row to position the seams in opposing directions. Join the rows. Press the seam allowances in one direction. The pieced quilt center should now measure 42½" square.

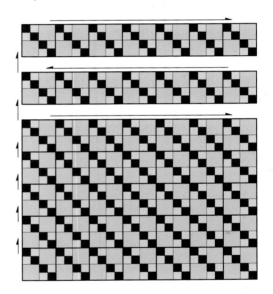

APPLIQUÉING THE BORDER STRIPS

1. With right sides together, fold a black print 9½" x 42½" strip in half crosswise and lightly press a center crease.

Center crease

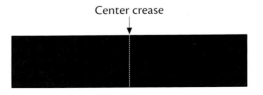

2. Referring to "Making Bias-Tube Stems and Vines" on page 13, prepare the medium-dark green print 1¼"-wide rectangles and strips.

3. Fold a prepared A appliqué in half and finger-press a center crease. Align the creases of the appliqué and the black border strip to center the vase, positioning the bottom of the vase approximately 1¼" up from the bottom border edge. Pin in place.

4. Referring to the illustration, lay out the vines on the border strip, ensuring that all raw ends are overlapped well where they intersect and join the vase. When you are pleased with their positions, dot the seam allowance of each vine with liquid basting glue and press it in place. Remove the vase. Referring to "Stitching the Appliqués" on page 15, stitch the stems in place.

PIN POINT

Duplicating Appliquéd Borders

Here's a quick trick for easily duplicating the design of appliquéd borders with a repeated design. Lay out, baste, and stitch your first border as desired. Next, lay the completed border strip on a carpeted area, smooth away any wrinkles, and lay the next strip to be appliquéd exactly over the top of the original piece. Use a water-soluble marker to gently trace along the raised edge of the vines and stems positioned below the top piece. This traced design will serve as a blueprint to duplicate the placement of the vines and stems, and once they are in place, filling in with the remaining appliqués is a snap.

5. Reposition, baste, and stitch the vase appliqué. Remove the paper pattern piece as instructed in "Removing Paper Pattern Pieces" on page 16.

6. Using the quilt photo as a guide, work from the bottom layer to the top to position, baste, and stitch the remaining B, C, D, E, E reversed, and F appliqués. Remember to remove the paper pattern pieces before adding each new layer. Please note that for the featured quilt, the E and E reversed appliqués were randomly positioned without regard to their direction and the pointed leaf ends were also randomly placed up or down for added interest.

7. Repeat steps 3–6 for a total of four appliquéd border strips.

ADDING THE BORDERS TO THE QUILT CENTER

1. Join an appliquéd border strip to the right and left sides of the quilt center. Carefully press the seam allowances toward the border strips, taking care not to apply heat to the appliqués.

2. Join a medium green 9½" square to each end of the remaining appliquéd border strips. Carefully press the seam allowances toward the black print. Join these pieced strips to the remaining sides of the quilt center. Carefully press the seam allowances toward the borders. The finished quilt top should measure 60½" square, including the seam allowances.

FINISHING THE QUILT

Refer to "Finishing Techniques" on page 19 for details as needed. Layer the quilt top, batting, and backing. Quilt the layers. The featured quilt was machine quilted with straight diagonal lines to form a crosshatch in the quilt center. The borders were quilted with a combination of echo quilting around the appliqués with an assortment of free-form shapes interspersed for interest. Squared feathered wreaths were quilted onto the border corner posts. Join the seven black print 2½" x 42" strips into one length and use it to bind the quilt.

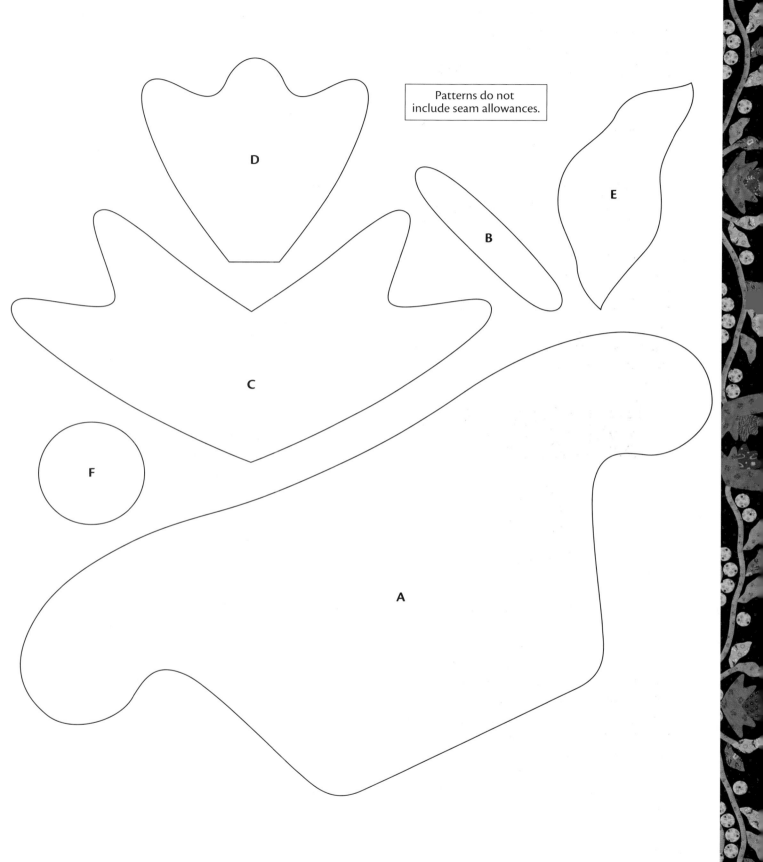

Patterns do not
include seam allowances.

D

B

E

C

F

A

Whirligigs

Remember days spent blowing on pinwheels and watching whirligigs turn in the summer breeze while you ran barefoot through Grandma's garden? Recapture those memories with some whirligigs of your own to be enjoyed throughout summer and beyond.

MATERIALS

4⅜ yards of cream print for background

7 fat quarters (18" x 22") of assorted brown prints for blocks and binding

7 fat quarters of assorted pink prints for blocks and binding

4 yards of fabric for backing

63" x 71" piece of batting

CUTTING

Cut all pieces across the width of the fabric unless otherwise noted.

From *each* of the 7 assorted brown and 7 assorted pink print fat quarters, cut:

16 rectangles, 2½" x 4½" (combined total of 224)

Enough 2½"-wide random lengths to make a 250" length of binding when joined end to end

From the cream print, cut:

56 strips, 2½" x 42"; crosscut into:
   448 squares, 2½" x 2½"
   224 rectangles, 2½" x 4½"

PIECING THE WHIRLIGIG BLOCKS

Sew all pieces with right sides together unless otherwise noted.

1. Lightly draw a diagonal line on the wrong side of each of the 448 cream print 2½" squares.

2. Select four matching brown print 2½" x 4½" rectangles. Layer a prepared cream print 2½" square over one end of each rectangle. Stitch the pairs together exactly on the drawn lines. Press and trim as instructed in "Pressing Triangle Units" on page 10. Repeat on the opposite end of each rectangle.

Make 4.

3. Join a cream print 2½" x 4½" rectangle to each of the pieced rectangles from step 2 to form a block unit. Press the seam allowances toward the cream print rectangle.

Make 4.

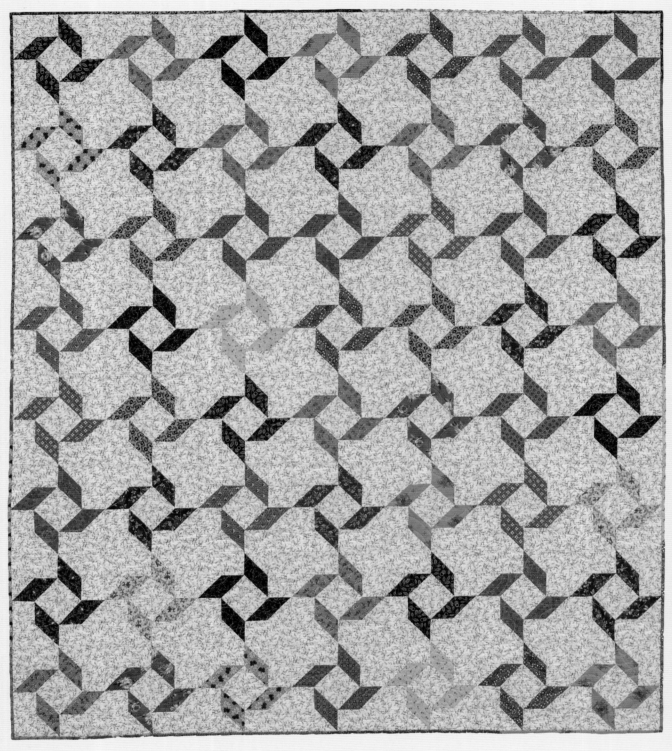

Finished quilt: 56½" x 64½" ■ Finished blocks: 8" x 8"
Designed by Kim Diehl. Pieced by Evelyne Schow and Pat Hansen. Machine quilted by Cynthia Fuelling.

4. Lay out four units as shown to make a Whirligig block. Join the pieces in each horizontal row. Press the seam allowances of the top row to the left; press the seam allowances of the bottom row to the right. Join the rows. Press the center seam allowances open.

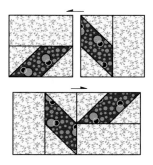 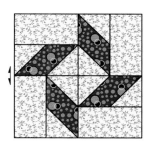

5. Repeat steps 2–4 for a total of 28 assorted pink blocks and 28 assorted brown blocks measuring 8½" square, including the seam allowances.

ASSEMBLING THE QUILT TOP

1. Lay out four brown blocks and three pink blocks in alternating positions. Join the blocks to make a row. Press the seam allowances toward the brown blocks. Repeat for a total of four A rows.

Row A.
Make 4.

2. Referring to step 1, use four pink blocks and three brown blocks to make a row. Repeat for a total of four B rows.

Row B.
Make 4.

3. Referring to the quilt photo, lay out four A rows and four B rows in alternating positions. Join the rows. Press the seam allowances in one direction. The pieced quilt top should measure 56½" x 64½", including the seam allowances.

COMPLETING THE QUILT

Refer to "Finishing Techniques" on page 19 for details as needed. Layer the quilt top, batting, and backing. Quilt the layers. The featured quilt was machine quilted in an overall swirling pattern as provided in "Machine Quilting" on page 20. Join the 2½"-wide random lengths of assorted pink and brown prints into one length and use it to bind the quilt.

Mocha Stars

What could be better than colorful stars floating in a sky of chocolaty goodness?
Broaden your horizons with these uniquely pieced and appliquéd stars, and then
dress them to perfection with twining vines of luscious blooms.

MATERIALS

For this project, I suggest choosing a variety of light, medium, and dark prints for the assorted fat quarters. Keep in mind that the majority of these prints should stand out well from your brown border print so that your appliqués don't become "lost."

18 fat quarters (18" x 22") of assorted prints for star, flower, and berry appliqués

2½ yards of brown print for border and binding

¾ yard of light tan print for block backgrounds

¾ yard of medium tan print for block backgrounds

½ yard of medium green print for stem and leaf appliqués

1 fat quarter of light green print for star, flower-center, and leaf appliqués

4 yards of fabric for backing

67" x 67" square of batting

⅜" bias bar

CUTTING

Cut all pieces across the width of the fabric unless otherwise noted. Refer to page 111 for appliqué patterns B–E and to "Invisible Machine Appliqué" beginning on page 10 for pattern piece preparation. You will cut the pattern A pieces later.

From the light tan print, cut:
2 squares, 20⅞" x 20⅞"; cut each square *once* diagonally to yield a total of 4 triangles

From the medium tan print, cut:
2 squares, 20⅞" x 20⅞"; cut each square *once* diagonally to yield a total of 4 triangles

From *each* of the 18 assorted print fat quarters, cut:
4 rectangles, 5" x 11" (combined total of 72)

From the remainder of the assorted print fat quarters, cut a *total* of:
13 using pattern B (large star centers and center vine intersection)

24 using pattern B (large flower centers)

72 using pattern C (flower petals) in matching sets of three, with one set to match each of the B flower-center appliqués

From the *bias* of the medium green print, cut:
4 strips, 1¼" x 12"

4 rectangles, 1¼" x 4½"

8 strips, 1¼" x 18"

8 strips, 1¼" x 8"

Finished quilt: 60½" x 60½" ■ Finished blocks: 20" x 20"
Designed, pieced, and machine appliquéd by Kim Diehl. Machine quilted by Celeste Freiberg.

From the remainder of the medium green print, cut:

24 using pattern D

24 using pattern D reversed

From the fat quarter of light green print, cut:

37 using pattern C

8 using pattern D

8 using pattern D reversed

From the *lengthwise grain* of the brown print, cut:

2 strips, 10½" x 40½"

2 strips, 10½" x 60½"

From the remaining brown print, cut:

7 strips, 2½" x 42" (binding)

PREPARING THE STAR APPLIQUÉS

The star appliqués are made up of left- and right-facing points, which can easily become reversed and result in appliqué pieces that don't fit together properly. The steps that follow will help simplify the preparation steps for these appliqués and help ensure they are facing in the correct direction as you make your blocks.

1. Lay a piece of freezer paper, waxy side down, over pattern A. Use a pencil and acrylic ruler to trace the shape. With the waxy sides together, layer this traced piece of paper over a second piece of freezer paper and use a hot, dry iron to fuse the pieces together. Use a rotary cutter and acrylic ruler to cut out the pattern template exactly on the drawn lines. As an added safeguard, align the cut template with the pattern provided in the project instructions to ensure it is facing in the correct direction and label the upper point with an "L" to indicate that this is the left-facing star point. Mark an X on the lower right-hand edge of the template.

2. Cut a long strip of freezer paper approximately 11" wide. Beginning with the *non-waxy* side of the paper facing up, fold the paper accordion-style at approximately 5" intervals. (A thickness of no more than eight folded layers will work best.)

3. Use the prepared pattern A template, with the "L" designation facing up, to trace the shape onto the topmost rectangle of folded freezer paper. Secure the layers with a straight pin or staple to prevent them from shifting and use a rotary cutter and acrylic ruler to cut out the pattern pieces exactly on the drawn lines.

4. *Before removing the pin or staple,* on the non-waxy side, label the upper point of the topmost pattern piece with an "L." Next, label the top non-waxy side of the next mirror-image piece with an "R" and continue in this manner until the top non-waxy paper side of each pattern piece in the stack has been labeled. In the same manner, work through the *bottom right-hand* edges of the stack to label the non-waxy paper side of each piece with an X. Remove the pin or staple and separate the pattern pieces into two stacks as shown. Repeat for a total of 36 left- and 36 right-facing star-point pattern pieces.

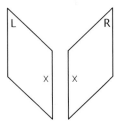

5. With the waxy side *down*, center a prepared pattern piece onto the *wrong* side of an assorted print 5" x 11" rectangle. Use a hot, dry iron to fuse the pattern piece in place. Repeat with the remaining pattern pieces for a total of 72 fused rectangles (36 left and 36 right).

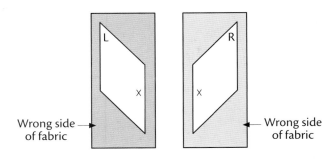

Wrong side of fabric → | ← Wrong side of fabric

6. Use a rotary cutter and acrylic ruler to cut out each fused star-point unit, adding a ¼" seam allowance on all sides as you cut. Reserve the fabric scraps that remain from each trimmed corner.

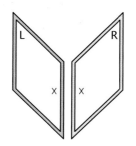

¼" seam allowance →

Make 36 of each.

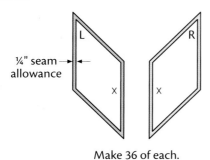

PIN POINT

Consistently Aligning Your Acrylic Ruler

When aligning the ¼" line of your acrylic ruler with the paper pattern piece edges of each star point, you can choose to position it directly over the paper edge, just *inside* the paper edge, or just *outside* the paper. Where you position this line isn't as important as positioning it consistently to ensure all of the pieces are uniform in size.

7. Select a prepared left and right star point unit. Lay the pieces out as shown, with the labeled paper sides facing up. With the fabric sides together, pin the pieces together along the edges that are marked with an X.

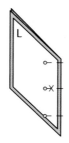

8. Starting at the top pinned paper edge and beginning with a couple of backstitches or a locking stitch, sew the pair together exactly next to the paper edge to make a quarter-star unit; *do not* sew above or below the paper pattern pieces. Remove the pins, *leaving the paper pattern pieces in place*. Do not press the seam allowances at this time.

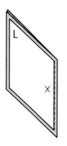

Do not sew beyond paper
at top and bottom edges.

9. Repeat steps 7 and 8 for a total of 36 pieced quarter-star units.

10. Select two pieced quarter-star units. Pin and stitch these units together as instructed in steps 7 and 8, keeping the placement of the left and right star points accurate. Repeat for a total of 16 half-star units.

11. Without removing the paper pattern pieces, press the *side* seam allowances of each half-star unit open, working from the top edge down to the bottom where the seams converge. Next, press the center seam allowances of each half-star unit and each quarter-star unit open. Don't worry if the seams don't lie perfectly flat where they converge at the bottom edge; they'll be trimmed away later. Reserve the remaining quarter-star units for later use.

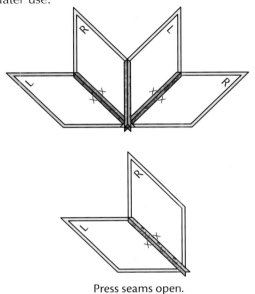

Press seams open.
Do not remove paper.

APPLIQUÉING THE STARS

1. Select a pieced half-star unit. Carefully peel away the freezer paper from each point. Reversing the direction of the paper pattern pieces so that the waxy sides are now facing *up*, reposition them onto the fabric, disregarding the "L" and "R" designations and sliding the paper under the pressed seam allowances until the pattern piece points are centered within the ¼" seam allowances of each fabric point. Carefully use the point of a hot, dry iron to re-press the patchwork seam allowances open onto the waxy side of the paper pattern pieces to anchor them in place.

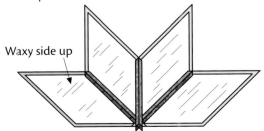

Waxy side up

2. Fold back the top portion of each pattern piece and apply a small amount of fabric glue stick to the center of the exposed non-waxy side of the paper; reposition the top of the pattern piece and press it in place against the fabric.

3. Referring to the "Pressing Appliqués" on page 12, work from right to left (or left to right if you are left-handed) around the half-star unit to press the seam allowance of each individual point onto the waxy side of the freezer paper. Do not press the long, straight raw edge along the bottom of the unit because it will be enclosed within the seam when the block is pieced together.

   NOTE: You'll find it helpful to trim the fabric "flag" at each pressed star point to a scant ¼" as you press them. Applying a small amount of fabric glue stick to the bottom layer of this trimmed fabric and using the point of an awl or stiletto to drag and manipulate it until it rests on the back side of the point will also simplify the process. I recommend using the point of a hot, dry iron to fuse the glue at the star points, anchoring them in place so they'll be well hidden from the front.

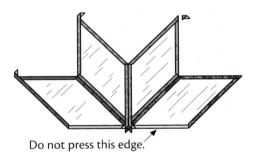

Do not press this edge.

4. Repeat steps 1–3 with the remaining half-star units and the reserved quarter-star units.

5. Select a light or medium tan print 20⅞" triangle, and with right sides together, carefully fold it in half from the center of the long bias edge to the point. Use a hot, dry iron to lightly press a center crease along the fold.

6. Position a prepared half-star unit onto the prepared triangle, with the center star seam aligned with the pressed background crease and the bottom raw edge flush with the bias edge of the triangle. Carefully fold back one half of the star unit at the center seam to expose the wrong side of one half of the star. Apply tiny dots of liquid basting glue along the outer pressed seam allowances *only* of the star points; do not apply glue to the sewn seams or paper pattern pieces. Reposition the glue-basted portion of the star and press it securely in place. Repeat with the remaining half of the star unit. Next, apply three or four *tiny* dots of liquid glue between the fabric layers of the star and triangle along the bottom edge where they rest together. From the wrong side of the prepared triangle, use a hot, dry iron to briefly press the star unit and heat set the glue. Trim away the dog-ear points of the star unit.

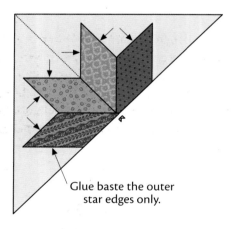

Glue baste the outer
star edges only.

7. Referring to "Stitching the Appliqués" on page 15, appliqué the star in place. Do not remove the paper pattern pieces at this time.

8. Repeat steps 5–7, using both the light and medium tan print triangles, to make a total of eight appliquéd triangles. Reserve the remaining half-star and quarter-star appliqué units for use in the border.

PIECING THE QUILT CENTER

Sew all pieces with right sides together unless otherwise noted.

1. Select a light and medium tan print appliquéd triangle. Join the triangles along the center diagonal edges, ensuring that the outer star edges

are aligned. (Please note that it isn't necessary to perfectly match up the center star seams because this portion of the block will later be covered with an appliqué.) Press the center block seam allowances open. Trim away the dog-ear points. Repeat for a total of four pieced and appliquéd star blocks measuring 20½" square, including the seam allowances.

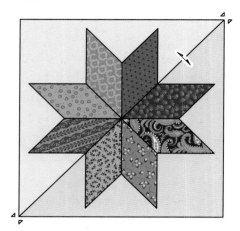

2. Referring to "Removing Paper Pattern Pieces" on page 16, cut away the background print underneath each star appliqué, leaving about a ½" seam allowance along the center block seam to grade it and reduce bulk. Carefully peel away the paper pattern pieces.

3. Referring to the quilt photo on page 104, lay out the star blocks in two rows of two blocks each, with the blocks positioned so that the background print colors are different where they meet. Join the blocks in each horizontal row. Press the seam allowances toward the medium tan print. Join the rows. Press the seam allowances to one side. The pieced quilt center should now measure 40½" square, including the seam allowances.

APPLIQUÉING THE QUILT CENTER

1. Referring to "Making Bias-Tube Stems and Vines" on page 13, prepare the medium green print 1¼"-wide bias strips and rectangles.

2. Referring to the quilt photo, dot the seam allowances of the 12" stems with glue and position them onto the quilt center where the block seams

intersect. In the same manner, anchor a 4½" stem on the outer corners of the quilt center, positioning it over the pressed diagonal block crease to perfectly center it (the bottom corner edges of each stem should rest on the raw edges of the block). Stitch the stems in place. Reserve the remaining prepared stems for use in the border.

3. From the reserved fabric scraps set aside in step 6 of "Preparing the Star Appliqués," cut a total of 40 using pattern E on page 111.

4. Gather the following prepared appliqués for the quilt center:

   - 8 assorted print matching flower sets consisting of one B appliqué and three C appliqués

   - 5 assorted print B appliqués for the large star centers and stem intersection

   - 13 light green print C appliqués for the small flower centers and small star centers

   - 24 medium and light green print D and D reversed appliqués

   - 8 assorted print E appliqués

5. Select a matching set of B and C appliqués. Referring to the quilt photo, position the B appliqué at the outermost end of a 12" stem, overlapping the stem at least ¼"; pin in place. Lay out three matching C appliqués to form flower petals, tucking them under the B appliqué to achieve the look you desire. Pin or baste the C appliqués in place; remove the B appliqué. Repeat this process for each of the 12" and 4½" stems.

6. Stitch the C appliqués to the background. Remove the paper pattern pieces. Reposition, baste, and stitch the B appliqués, including one additional B appliqué for the quilt center where the stems intersect. Remove the paper pattern pieces.

7. Referring to the quilt photo, lay out and baste 24 prepared D and D reversed appliqués along the 12" and 4½" stems. Position and baste 13 light green C appliqués on the star and flower centers. Last, position and baste eight assorted print E appliqués. Stitch each appliqué in place and remove the paper pattern pieces.

APPLIQUÉING THE BORDER STARS

1. Fold each brown print 10½" x 40½" border strip in half crosswise, right sides together, and lightly press a vertical center crease along the fold. Repeat with the brown print 10½" x 60½" strips. For the 60½" strips *only*, measure 20" out from each side of the center crease and lightly press two additional creases.

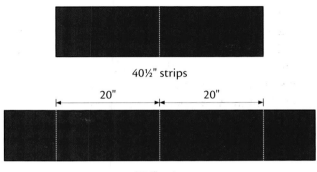

40½" strips

60½" strips

2. Select a prepared 10½" x 40½" border strip and position a reserved half-star appliqué unit onto it, with the center star seam aligned with the center crease of the strip and the raw edges flush. Glue baste the star unit in place as previously instructed. Repeat with each of the remaining 40½" and 60½" border strips.

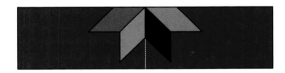

3. Position and baste a quarter-star appliqué unit on each end of the two 40½"-long border strips, aligning the raw edges as shown. Appliqué the quarter-star units and half-star units in place, leaving a small opening at each inner corner of the quarter-star units for adding the vines.

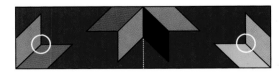

Leave small opening at each inner corner.

4. Position and baste two half-star appliqué units onto each 60½"-long border strip, aligning the center star seams with the remaining border creases. Appliqué each of the half-star appliqué units in place.

5. Stay stitch the long raw edges of the star units to the border strips, just inside the edges, and trim away the dog-ear points. Remove the paper pattern pieces, leaving a ½" seam allowance along the stay-stitched edges to grade the seams and reduce bulk.

ADDING THE BORDERS

Referring to the quilt photo, join an appliquéd 10½" x 40½" border strip to the right and left sides of the quilt center. Carefully press the seam allowances toward the border, taking care not to apply heat to the appliqués. In the same manner, join the 10½" x 60½" appliquéd border strips to the remaining sides of the quilt center, ensuring that the stars are aligned along their outer edges. Again, it is not necessary to perfectly match up the center star seams because they will be covered with appliqués. Carefully press the seam allowances toward the border. The pieced quilt top should now measure 60½" square, including the seam allowances.

COMPLETING THE APPLIQUÉ

1. Referring to the quilt photo, lay out and glue baste two medium green print 18"-long stems in each corner of the quilt top, tucking the raw ends into the star openings at least ¼". Add an 8"-long stem to each 18"-long stem as shown, ensuring that the raw ends are well tucked under the stems where they meet. Appliqué the stems and star openings.

2. Referring to step 5 of "Appliquéing the Quilt Center" on page 108, position a matching set of B and C flower appliqués at the end of each stem, positioning the B appliqués over the quilt seams to easily center them. Work from the bottom layer to the top to baste and stitch each appliqué as previously instructed. Remember to remove the paper pattern pieces before adding each new layer.

3. Referring to the quilt photo, for each forked set of vines radiating out from the border corner stars, lay out, baste, and stitch:

   • 2 light green print C appliqués for the small flower centers

   • 5 medium and light green print D and D reversed appliqués

   • 4 assorted print E appliqués

   Remember to remove the paper pattern pieces after the appliqué is complete.

4. Working from the bottom layer to the top, stitch an assorted print B appliqué and a light green print C appliqué to the center of each star in the border, remembering to remove the paper pattern pieces between each layer. To properly position the appliqués for the half-star units resting on the outer edge of the border, fold each prepared appliqué circle in half and finger-press a center crease. Position these circles on the stars with the pressed creases resting ¼" in from the raw star edge. After the appliqués have been stitched, trim away the excess B and C appliqué fabric that extends beyond the border edge and remove the paper pattern pieces.

COMPLETING THE QUILT

Refer to "Finishing Techniques" on page 19 for details as needed. Layer the quilt top, batting, and backing. Quilt the layers. The triangular block backgrounds of the featured quilt were stitched with a pebbled design and McTavishing, with each design placed consistently onto the same prints to emphasize the secondary block pattern. Each individual star point was quilted with a feathered stem. The open background areas of the border were stitched with a McTavishing design. Join the seven brown print 2½" x 42" strips into one length and use it to bind the quilt.

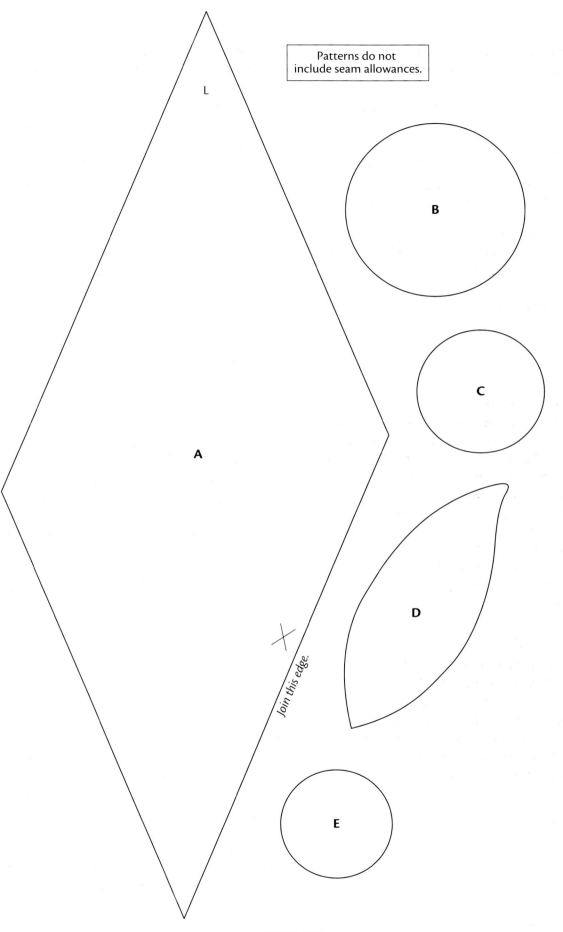

Patterns do not include seam allowances.

L

B

A

C

D

Join this edge.

E

About the Author

With just the third quilt she'd ever made, self-taught quilt-maker Kim Diehl entered and won *American Patchwork and Quilting* magazine's "Pieces of the Past" quilt challenge in 1998. This win took her life down a new and unexpected path, and with her fourth quilt, Kim began publishing her original designs.

In the years since her challenge win, Kim has seen her work published in numerous national and international magazines. In 2004, she began writing her best-selling "Simple" series of quilting books for Martingale & Company.

The opportunity to begin designing fabrics for Henry Glass in 2008 enabled Kim to combine her love of richly hued prints with her "scrap-basket" approach to quiltmaking, and her fabric designs reflect this. "My goal is for my fabric designs to work together beautifully without looking as though they were created together. What could be more fun than design-ing a quilt, and then creating the fabrics to bring it alive?" This endeavor has been especially rewarding for Kim because she has no formal artistic training and loves seeing where her natural instincts lead her.

Kim makes her home in scenic Idaho surrounded by her family, her much-spoiled pooches, and her country-style gardens. When she's not designing quilts and fabric, sewing patchwork, and working in her fragrant flower beds, Kim travels extensively around the country, teaching her easy invisible-machine-appliqué methods and sharing her quilts.